The long watch

The long watch

The long watch

Charles Allen Smart

The World Publishing Company · *Cleveland and New York*

Published by The World Publishing Company
2231 West 110th Street, Cleveland, Ohio 44102

Published simultaneously in Canada by
Nelson, Foster & Scott Ltd.

First printing 1968

Copyright © 1968 by Margaret W. H. Smart

Library of Congress Catalog Card Number: 68–13712

Printed in the United States of America

To Peggy

Introduction

Charles Allen Smart died in Chillicothe on March 11, 1967, after a short illness. However, just before his death he received the very welcome news that his war reminiscences had been accepted by The World Publishing Company. This information arrived on his last day of consciousness and gave him great satisfaction as he hated to think that he had spent months writing a book that no one wanted to read.

We talked cheerfully all that afternoon in his hospital room about *The Long Watch,* and I could see how great was his pleasure in knowing that this book would one day be available in print.

He began to write the book principally because of the urgings of his friend, Judge William Brown, and his nephew, George Dartt. They had been after him for years to put down on paper the experiences he had talked about so vividly.

After finishing *Viva Juárez!* he wrote various short pieces but couldn't seem to settle down to a book until he decided: "I might finally return to my experiences in the war—naturally among the most vivid and important in my life—and write these chapters in autobiography, which I might be said to have begun in several of my other books. During the war I had written to my wife almost daily, and she had saved all of these letters, without which I could not have undertaken this job. Because these letters had been censored by officers when I was an enlisted man, and more carefully by myself after I had been commissioned, they had a good many vague spots that I could not fill in from memory, so I took the trouble of checking my text against the logs, many in my own handwriting, now in the National Archives. However even many of these logs had been censored, presumably by the ONI. Because I am more interested in factual narratives of the war than in any fictions about it, and because I wanted to give the credit by name to many undecorated and unrecorded heroes I had known, I used proper names and pulled few punches, although there was almost no man whom I could not remember without basic sympathy."

Allen felt strongly how regrettable it was that only wars force people to give their best for their country.

MARGARET HUSSEY SMART

Barnstable, Massachusetts
October 20, 1967

Introduction 2

I am so glad this book is to be published. CAS was my brother-in-law and one of my favorite people. I miss our long talks and I miss his letters. We wrote to each other, talked endlessly, thought very much alike.

He was a shy man who loved people. Possibly, "love" isn't the word. He was interested in people and wanted to know what made them what they were. This comes through in his book. In enduring, at his age, the hardships of a life to which he was completely unaccustomed, he became fascinated by the men alongside whom he was fighting and working. He never meant to be critical, he was only being analytical. He wasn't writing a superficial and anecdotal account of those grim years. He was deeply interested in the reason for wars as well as being concerned with the men who fought them.

Being completely sincere himself, he detested insincerity in others. I think one reason for his deep love for my sister was his admiration of her because she was such an individual. He hated false snobbery, pretentiousness, foolish chitchat. He disliked seeing people waste their lives.

He was a good storyteller. Many nights we were fascinated by his tales of the war years and we begged him to write them down. Possibly, he didn't do this earlier because so many memoirs were then being published by those who seemed more important. He wasn't sure that anyone would be interested in the comparatively insignificant account of daily life aboard a ship. I think he was also afraid that his abrupt comments might hurt feelings. He could be very caustic, but this only demonstrated his impatience with hypocrisy.

CAS would have been the first to say that he was no great hero. He just wanted to get the job done and return to Peggy and Oak Hill. But he knew there was a job to be done.

EMILY HUSSEY HASKELL

Moosup, Connecticut
October, 1967

The long watch

1

When the experiences of a few moments or years sink deeply into our minds and remain actively alive there, sometimes they finally demand scrutiny, a search for significant details, insights, and meanings that may keep those experiences from being destructive or wasted. This little book about some of my experiences in the United States Navy in World War II is the result of such a search. Because I like firsthand documents more than most fictions, and because I knew many unsung heroes, I have named names and stuck as closely as a veteran can to the facts. Lest anyone be deceived, I hasten to state clearly that my experiences were in no way dramatic or heroic. Whatever interest and value this book may have will come from a distillation of experiences entirely too common in our century.

At the age of thirty-seven, on May 18, 1942, I enlisted as an Apprentice Seaman. After going to several camps and schools, I served on three different LSTs (Landing Ships Tank or "Large, Slow Targets"): first in the New Guinea campaign; then in the English Channel, including D-Day; and finally again in the Pacific, arriving at Okinawa just as that island was secured. In my first two ships I served as an enlisted man, first as a signalman, then as a quartermaster, rising to Chief Quartermaster. Then I was commissioned a Lieutenant (jg) and made Executive Officer of my last ship. Later I was promoted to full Lieutenant, and for six days until I was relieved at my own request—the war having ended and my points being sufficient—I was Commanding Officer of that last ship. Then I was sent back to the States, and on September 28, 1945, I was released.

Of course millions of men and women lived through all this or very much more, trying only to do their jobs as well as they could and to get somehow to the end of it. Except as one submicroscopic part of the whole effort, I myself made few sacrifices and did nothing important or glamorous. I saw some action in both oceans, but in most cases we arrived after others had made the situation relatively safe—assuming for the moment that there is such a thing as relative safety, in war or peace. Like all the other men on my ships while I was aboard them, I was never scratched by the enemy. I received no decoration and deserved none. Each of my three tours overseas lasted only about eight months, and I got home every year. At the end I still had a hernia from lifting cases of ammunition in New Orleans, and I was so exhausted that I was near some kind of a mental collapse, but I consider these "wounds" both educational and relatively unimportant and lucky. Since the former "wound" was in my groin, and since I too have probably talked too much about the war, I might be called Uncle Toby.

For me and probably for others, all of it was then and is now a kind of surrealistic dream. Waiting and then traveling endlessly to destinations we rarely knew in advance, we lived in a world apart, unlike any world most of us had ever known. For the most part we lived in extremes of exertion, pressure, discipline, and boredom. We suffered more from lack of sleep than from anything else, including the fear of death. Next we suffered most (and this fact has

been too generally ignored) from lack of confidence in ourselves and in those above and below us in rank and responsibility. This anxiety was exacerbated by our living very
tightly and dependently together in danger while most of
us were trying to make a taut ship and do a good job. Our
sense of time became confused and blurred, and the past
as unreal as the future, so that we came to doubt that we
had ever lived, or ever should live, in any other way. All
this was broken and relieved by having to learn new jobs
hard and fast; by sudden and weird changes of fortune; by
friendships and hatreds that were both deep and ephemeral; by humor and comedy, low and higher; by glimpses,
in the sea, the skies, the ships, the coasts and islands, the
shattered cities, and the minds of men under pressure, of
great beauty, and by other glimpses into the depths of evil
and horror.

This was a fair share of living for a period of three years
and four months, and it has affected my life for good and
ill ever since, but for twenty years I have been wondering
just what its basic meanings were for me and possibly for
others today who are less interested than I am in the Navy
and in those "battles long ago." By *meanings* I mean here
something less intellectual and moral than artistic and
emotionally penetrating.

As I think now of those thousands of men I saw involved with each other in war at sea, everywhere between
New Guinea and Normandy, and of that long series of
quite implausible events in which I took part, what strikes
me most strongly is that these men had very little understanding or control, either of themselves or of the great
events that were battering and sweeping them onward; and
that nevertheless, laughing, cursing, and wondering, they
tried to do as well as they could the jobs to which their
deepest loyalties and the tricks of fate had committed

them. What strikes me next is that except for the intolerable destruction, waste, and stupidity of war, and except for the differences in the nature and degree of the pressures put upon us, the situation is much the same for all of us in times of relative peace. Precisely because it is hopeless, doomed, and absurd, any little effort, however small and ephemeral, to live fully and well while we can, to bring love and craftsmanship to the making of our own little worlds, is an end in itself. It gives some meaning and beauty to history, and it laughs at the galaxies. It can be deepened and decorated, but also corrupted, by education and religion. However obscure and ineffective, any such effort is a work of art, bringing briefly a little light and order into the chaos. We can see instances of it all around us, every day.

In this situation, although too often we lack his ingenuity and grace, his humility and dignity, we are all, including the great, very much like Charlie Chaplin's little tramp. In France more than thirty years ago, I was happy when my French friends called me Charlot. Here then is a record of one little tramp fumbling his way, among better and less lucky men, through that war at sea of twenty-odd years ago. With his mates and with the human race, he may provide a little ironic but compassionate laughter.

2

On a clear, cold Sunday in December 1941, my wife and I went on a picnic with friends to a gravel plant they owned on a bank high above a river in southern Ohio. We had a good meal, cooked outdoors, and then amused ourselves (with odd appropriateness) by firing pistols and a rifle at bottles that we tossed into the river upstream. While we were doing this, a man came running down the C & O track that ran through the plant, and our host recognized him as the signalman from a nearby railroad tower. This man excitedly told us of the Japanese attack on the fleet in Pearl Harbor. The next day, we sat near the radio in our dining room, listening to the President address Congress and then to the national anthem. At the end, I said: "That's really a requiem, for all the dead." Peggy said: "Yes, and I hope not for us." Then I quoted banally, as many others must have done: " 'Never send to know for whom the bell tolls. . . .' "

Who can forget those moments, those years? Evidently a good many tourists have. They tell me that the Japanese are very artistic and courteous, that the Germans are very clean and hard-working. I believe them, but I also remember.

It was now a question, far from unexpected but put now imperatively, of my deepest loyalties.

My wife and I had been given much by our country, as

well as by chance, and we knew it. In Cleveland and New York, and especially during summers with my aunt at Oak Hill, the old family place in southern Ohio, I had had a happy childhood in which reading and writing were considered essential pleasures, all people and animals worthy of respectful attention, and boredom a dull kind of folly. When I went to Harvard I continued reading and writing among teachers and students more brilliant than myself; and I was also able, in those days, to do my share of loafing and inviting my callow but curious soul. After bumbling about wide-eyed in New York as a book editor and freelance hack, I wrote my first novel (green but clever and promising, like so many) and on the royalties was able to live happily in Europe, mostly in France, for more than a year, on about two dollars a day. Naturally, there was now no hope of my ever being a substantial citizen, or anything but a writer. In France I wrote my second novel, a neat, Gallic job of writing but it was unfortunately about love, a matter in which my interest far exceeded my knowledge. It was published just when the banks were closed by the Depression, but it really didn't deserve a better fate; and by this time, with fantastic good luck, I had got a job teaching English at the Choate School.

When my aunt died and left me and my sister Oak Hill, another small farm, and a little money, I decided to give up the life of Mr. Chips and try to earn my living, while also writing, as a farmer. Soon after, I married a New England girl who had been similarly fortunate in her youth, and who took to our now rugged life with zest and skill. Cattle were selling at less than five cents a pound, but I wrote a book about our experiences, *R.F.D.*, that after four years without such amenities brought us plumbing, a furnace, a tractor, and a wash drawing by Andrew Wyeth. I also wrote two other books that were among my best but were largely ignored until gasoline rationing forced the public to buy and read almost anything. By this time I had learned something about farming, the New Deal and the war in Europe had raised farm prices, and I had an able and energetic younger partner in my farm operations. We expanded and actually began to make money, but were so active that I began to wonder whether I should have to give up either farming or writing.

To the perceptive, this conflict was probably implicit in my appearance and interests. When dressed for town, I seem to have had a tweedy-Harvard-schoolmaster look, if on the messy side; yet I was happy and effective in muddy dungarees, with a shovel, even if I did sometimes lean on it and contemplate the landscape. For a year I wore a beard, General Grant style, like my grandfather's, and because Communists hunted me down, as a liberal, articulate Democrat, and I liked to argue with them, my beard was long remembered with suspicion by some of my more limited neighbors. However, the farmers, I think, had come to like and respect me, as indeed I did them, while the ancestry of my wife and myself, and our handsome old stone house, inclined the other provincial "aristocrats" to try at least to overlook my political views and my agnosticism. For years, however, and in good company, I was blackballed by the gentlemen's discussion club in the town. These matters did not much interest us. As a farmer's wife, a passionate gardener, and a Girl Scout leader, Peggy had her hands and mind full, as I did, with such diverse matters as the reason ewes sometimes disowned their lambs, George Santayana's doctrine of essence, the corn-hog ratio, and—increasingly and depressingly—the threats from Europe and the Pacific.

Sometimes I have wondered idly what might have happened to me if the United States had somehow escaped the war. I might have become a kind of William Morris of the corn belt. If I had stayed on the farm during the war, I suspect that I might well have suffered, secretly, a mental wound, withdrawn into my farms and myself, become successful but wretched as a farmer, and written little or nothing more.

As it was, along with almost all other lucky young Americans, I felt that I now had a clear call and opportunity to pay for my country's gifts to me by giving her all my time and energies and risking my neck for her. I must also admit to having had another motive that was less normal and perhaps less creditable. As a writer, I was immensely curious about warfare as one of the experiences of most of the men of my savage century, and I didn't see how I could fully understand them, or expect them to listen to me, if I had not shared that experience.

Yet my decision was not as easy as this may sound. Months later, my doubts were expressed more vividly than I could have expressed them by a shipmate who said to me: "Christ, Charlie, what is this fucking war all about? Oh! I know; we don't like to be pushed around, or to see other little bastards being pushed around. O.K., and I'm glad to be here, but why do these fuckers have to do it? This sort of shit has been going on forever. It goes on at home. What does all this fucking, bloody history add up to? Hell! I ain't heard one good answer yet."

I didn't have one easy, all-embracing, convincing answer then, and I don't have one now. It may be that the only answer is that just such questions are being asked by the people who are the growing edge of mankind. The key question is "Why do these fuckers have to do it?"—and why do they find so much support? I'm afraid that beneath all the obvious and partly true answers—power-politics, profit-hunger, obsolete nationalism, ideologies, misguided idealism, boredom, plain hunger, and all the rest—there is a sickness to some degree present in every soul: a willingness to kill and be killed in defense of our egos rather than to trust our deeper selves in loving human life, and to risk more on that love. The essence of all history is the effort of the more healthy, loving people to get more control of themselves and of the situation, naturally by means as little violent as possible. Until they get control of most of the nations and weapons, I see no hope in any political solution, and on the record I see no hope for the necessary upsurge of health, love, and intelligence as a result of any form of religion or even education with which I am familiar.

As a result of this attitude, before, during, and since that war I have had seizures of disgust, despair, and total pacifism. (I have never been able to accept the distinction and compromise of the Friends, who served as medical men with such notable courage.) Even after Pearl Harbor, I asked myself whether my gratitude to my country, my curiosity about war, and my wish to be respected by my friends and neighbors were not all leading me into a timid acquiescence and cooperation as shameful as that of the Germans. Of these seizures I was cured in part by the detachment advocated in the *Bhagavad-Gita,* but much more by trying to imagine what would happen to my country and the world if enough of us Americans were pacifists to cripple the war effort and result in our subjugation by the barbarians. I could foresee nothing but a longer, more terrible underground war in which I should find myself taking part. Alternatively, if others won the war while I sat it out in a camp for conscientious objectors, I could not then live with myself or anyone else. Also, some nations were more obsolete and dangerous than others, and the United States, Britain, and France, even as fighting nations, seemed to me the only hope of any people relatively civilized.

I have not yet changed these views. Our victory in that war was a victory for decency; we have had twenty years of peace of sorts, and if we keep our heads clear and our hearts warm and do not indulge in religious wars, the dead in that war will not have died in vain. Even the new weapons have been effective, so far, in limiting wars, and in time enough people may become so frightened by them, and so disgusted by their waste, as to permit the creation of a strong and democratic world state that could stop major wars and even increase freedom and justice.

Even after I had got rid of my bouts of pacifism, I felt for some time serious doubts about intervention. At that time we had numerous callers who tried to convert me to this or that, and I remember saying to an Englishman, "Look! I remember that we finished one world war 'to make the world safe for democracy,' and what good did that do? We Americans are not world-minded, and we are not omnipotent. I doubt very much that we would or could follow through another victory into world leadership, and into stopping all this bloody nonsense." He said, "You have no choice, and you are wasting your time." I said, "Maybe not. How do you know that the wool on that sheep's back may not go into a uniform on an Englishman's back, or on my own?"

However, the collapse of the French army and government, the heroic resistance of the English under the bombings, and the inklings or more at that time about the fate of the Jews in Germany all moved me further from such calculations. Our true loves can only be extended gradually, and our men have fought and died in Korea, Vietnam, and elsewhere, largely as a result of calculations and more orders that I consider sound, which makes the thoughtful among them more heroic, but western Europe was and is for me something else again. Some months before Pearl Harbor I was an open interventionist and my wife and I were active in the local work of Bundles for Britain. By December 7, 1941, I was wholly committed, and the attack came almost as a relief.

3

Like many others, I had my troubles in getting into the service in some reasonable manner, and both my wife and I found the five months between Pearl Harbor and my enlistment almost as difficult as any five months after that.

Our farming operation was not a large one, but there could be no question of liquidating any farming operation during a war. Luckily, I had at that time an excellent farm partner named Orley Anderson. He spent part of his time on a job, I spent part of my time writing, and we both spent all the rest of our time farming two small farms. When I pulled out, he gave up his job to farm full time, and because he had two children as well as a wife, he reluctantly decided to accept—he had to—the exemption from the draft allowed to one man by the size of our farming operation. He and his family moved into our home with my wife, and later he moved to our other farm, which we sold to him. Thanks to the good sense of the Andersons and my wife, this difficult adjustment was made very well, but like every other sailor, I had my worries about hardships and complexities at home. One of the ironies was that while I came through three campaigns with hardly a scratch, Orley Anderson worked so hard on the farms that he suffered a severe heart attack—and of course got no government compensation for injuries in work that was as important as mine, and less glamorous. Soon after I enlisted, my wife Peggy got a job under the local rationing board, and later she went to live with her brother and his family in California and got a job in a bank there. Once when I came home from boot camp the head of the rationing board told me that, to him, Peggy was worth her weight in gold. It takes the whole nation to win or prevent a war.

Suspecting my own interest in the Navy and a uniform, I investigated jobs in the Department of Agriculture, but soon decided that I didn't want to join the group of men I met there, all of whom were horribly frustrated because they could not, for various reasons, get into any branch of the armed forces.

During my college years I had worked one summer in a merchant ship as a deck cadet, but when I thought of going into merchant ships again, primarily for the good pay to send home to Peggy, she put her foot down, for the first and last time. Our merchant ships were being blown up and sunk all over the world, and she said that she simply would not allow me to go out and get killed just for *money*. Besides, she pointed out correctly, the government took care of its men during and after wars. So I gave up that idea.

I know that the merchant seamen did a dangerous and essential job, without glamor, but I also remember the anger and contempt that most of us in the Navy felt for them, because of things like this. In Milne Bay the men of a naval armed guard in a merchant ship, who were not allowed to touch anything but their guns, told us that when a merchant seaman ran up the ensign on a Sunday he got fifty cents overtime pay! Because of its actions that seemed to me equally unpatriotic and greedy, I finally wrote home to Peggy to resign for me from my own union of sorts, the Farm Bureau.

While I was in Washington to visit the Department of Agriculture, I also loked up an officer I knew in the Navy Department, and he sent me around to the heavily guarded rooms devoted to codes. There I was interviewed by an Ensign who was so pale and nervous that he scared me about his work. In breaking the Japanese codes, those men had a major part in winning the battle of Midway, one of the most critical in the Pacific war. I wonder how many of them arrived in mental hospitals. This Ensign told me that they would mail to me, one at a time, four classified though of course elementary exercises or problems in breaking codes. If I solved all four of these, I'd be made an Ensign and put to work in those rooms. During the following weeks, I neglected my farm jobs and spent hours, day and night, working on those problems in cryptanalysis. I solved the first three, then got stuck in the fourth, which was properly much harder than the others. It kept me awake at night, and finally, about three one morning, I had an idea for a new attack on it. I went to work on graph paper on the floor of my study, and I may have come too close to solving that one because that night I decided that I simply could not endure working on such stuff, in those guarded rooms, for the duration. I went back to bed, and the next day I wrote to my ghostly officers that I was unable to solve No. 4.

Next I heard that if I went to New York, I could reasonably apply there for a commission in combat intelligence in the aircraft carriers. After waiting all one day in offices jam-packed with applicants, I was interviewed at length and then told that if I presented all the required documents, and if I passed both the medical examination and an investigation by the Office of Naval Intelligence, I'd be commissioned a Lieutenant. I was given a medical examination, and as far as I could tell I passed it. I could not imagine myself as a Lieutenant aboard a carrier, but

I decided that that worry was the Navy's. I went home in a more cheerful state of mind than I had known since December 7. One gray afternoon weeks later, when I was drenching my sheep for worms, Peggy came out to the barn and handed me a letter from the Navy Department that informed me, in the brusque and formal naval manner, that I had been denied a commission for unspecified "medical reasons." This plunged me again into gloom and also baffled me, because after eight years of farming I felt in better physical condition that I had known before in my life, or have known since. Years later, I heard a story that I had been denied a commission because a neighbor had told an investigating officer from ONI that I was a dangerous Red. This troubled me seriously for a while, but in the end I did not believe it, or much care.

Often during these months, despite the opinions of officer friends that I should be stupidly wasting myself, I had thought of simply enlisting in the Navy, and had been deterred only by the low wages of enlisted men. Even with her job and our recent small profits from farming, Peggy would be pinched more than I considered justifiable by my curiosity and patriotism.

At this point, however, money again entered the picture in the odd, ironic, amusing, and decisive manner that I find characteristic of its operations. In a move then quite legitimate, intended to spare her children inheritance taxes when she died, Peggy's mother gave to each of them a sum of money and entered into contracts with them and their spouses for the payment to her of most of the income from these sums when invested. Although Peggy was now almost as dependent on me as she had been before, I didn't see how I could legally claim that she was and, while panting to get into service, I didn't intend to put up an argument why I should be kept out of it. At the time the draft law had been passed, I had registered for it on almost the

last day on which, because of my age, I could have been
required to do so, and I had drawn a very low number. I
now reported that I no longer had a dependent and was
promptly put into Class 1-A. I still wanted to ride to my
work in a ship, and with Peggy's full agreement, I enlisted
in the Navy.

As will be apparent, after these months of painful groping and fumbling, I was very lucky in finding myself on
just the right track, but at that time and since, many men
have not been so lucky, and this is wasteful for them and
for their country. I should like to see seriously studied and
proposed some plan of universal service, for both men and
women, military or civil (but equally severe), for two years
immediately after high school, followed by longer, less
active service in the appropriate reserve organizations.
This could be tied in with Civil Defense, which as now
conceived and operated seems to me unrealistic. Well conceived and administered, some such plan would not, I
hope, require or result in any kind of a police state, and
it might help us all to more active and effective citizenship
throughout adult life.

There was a week's delay before I was sent off, and—besides the natural emotions of such a time—we had the embarrassment of publicity in local and other Ohio newspapers
about the enlistment of a "well-known writer." Nuts.

When I had passed the final medical examination with
no trouble and, standing in a group of about twenty boys
in the federal building in Cincinnati, repeated the oath, my
relief was again great. As millions of men and women
know, however, it is a bit of a jolt, comparable to that experienced by anyone who has said "I do" in a marriage
ceremony. During the three and a half years that followed,
it occurred to both Peggy and myself more than once that
military service by married people is a form of bigamy.

4

When I enlisted, an old officer of the Rainbow Division told me that I'd find life as a "gentleman ranker"—his and Kipling's phrase, not mine—easier if I always did three things: (1) did what I was told to do; (2) kept my mouth shut; and (3) kept my eyes and mind open. Although I did not always follow this advice, I found it excellent. When a five-star General grew too big for his fancy hat, forgot these precepts, and was sacked by the President, I was one of the millions of veterans, perhaps chiefly former sailors, who rejoiced. There is one important respect in which all persons in the armed forces are equal.

In my sixteen years since college, my life had not been sheltered, but my memories of boot camp at Great Lakes remind me of the time when I dove from a ketch into the icy waters off the coast of Maine. We were stripped naked and given strange new clothes that weren't fitted for days and that we had to spend almost every spare moment washing. We were given endless inoculations—although not, as the veterans of three days warned us, in the left nut —and these always brought back the severe colds from which all suffered almost steadily. Our Chiefs, whom we had to salute and call "Sir," were not sailors but former athletes, the "Tunneyfish" who ran us in formation, miles and miles, wherever we had to go: to get more shots, or to go to the dentist, or to take more mental tests, or to go to

church services, or to listen to name bands and sing "Don't
Sit Under the Apple Tree," and "Deep in the Heart of
Texas." On the occasions when we merely marched, we
had to sing "Anchors Aweigh" or "Everybody Loves the
Navy of the U.S.A."—a very dubious proposition. Every
day, besides washing our clothes and rolling and stowing
them properly, we had to clean and polish the decks, walls,
and windows of our barracks. (*"Keerist!"* said one lad. "I
thought Mom was fussy!") The food was good and plenti-
ful, but it seemed less so to me after hours and days of
"mess-cooking," which means running around after the
cooks, cleaning up everything, hauling garbage, and so on.
We drilled for hours with rifles that we never used again,
and we even marched in a huge parade in Chicago, in
which the man at the mike on the reviewing stand announced our wretched little company, out of step between
two bands, as "Now, folks, *here* come the heroic survivors
of the *Yorktown!*"

Of course we spent hours, day and night, rigorously
standing watches that had no purpose whatever except the
reasonable one of getting us mentally used to standing
watches and going without sleep. We slept, when we could,
in hammocks strung fiddle-string tight between jack-stays
about five feet above the deck. When you managed to get
into one, you lay there rigid like the filling of a cigar, because if you moved at all, you rolled out and found yourself stunned on the deck. Often at night petty officers
would come around to test the tightness of the hammocks
or merely to have their own kind of fun by dumping sleeping boots onto the deck. If anyone murmured the slightest
protest, he carried his full seabag, lashed into his ham-
mock, for hours. The obvious and necessary purpose of all
this was to get us into some kind of physical shape, to
make severe cleanliness a habit, to make sleep a luxury

rather than a right, to find out whether we had brains enough to go to different schools, and above all to beat permanently out of our heads any slight resistance to authority or any vagrant notion that we existed at all, or had any right to exist, except as working units at the bottom of the Navy.

Looking back at all this later from the ships, I thought it made good sense in general, but that all the drilling with and without rifles, and especially the parades, were somewhat wasteful in view of our total ignorance of ships and seamanship, of which a good deal can be taught and learned on land. We had a few hours of marlinespike seamanship, but not nearly enough, and after our absurd one hour in whaleboats on the lake, we agreed that our only hope lay in lifebelts. It would have been better if we had been shoved around by real sailors, but of course none of these could be spared from the ships, and since this was so, the Tunneyfish idea was not a bad one. Our own Chief was an Italian ex-social worker and athlete named S. J. Cavallaro, who was much more humane and intelligent than most of his colleagues. At the time, I lost my mustache and ten pounds and ran around in a wondering and only slightly resentful daze.

Even the few liberties that were given us had that quality of unreality. In my experience, the people of Chicago were always imaginatively kind to us, but in our new sailor-suits we still felt like phoneys who had wandered out into the streets from a theatre. We had not yet acquired the savvy, and the somber acceptance of loneliness, of old sailors on liberty. Very kind friends of my family took me into their homes, and there I discovered that I had enjoyed comfort, fine food, and above all manners and good talk, all my life, without quite knowing it. However, in these homes I also encountered some naval officers and discovered from their embarrassment and mine, for all their courtesy, that now I was no longer a "gentleman." My worst embarrassment came when a new, very young Ensign who had had too many drinks took me aside, told me that he was terrified of gunfire and of the sea, and burst into tears! All I could say was that we all felt the same, and that it was not at all surprising or important. The big moment and the wonderful hours came when Peggy managed to get herself to Chicago, but in those days neither of us had got used to being a sailor and his wife, together for a few hours and then torn apart. When I got home for a few hours, I was deeply moved by my home and countryside and by the welcome of old friends, but already I felt like a stranger from a very different world, almost a Lazarus.

None of my mates in boot camp had been as privileged as I had been, but all of us had been much more free and proud than we had known we were, and to find ourselves prisoners and worms, pushed around by men who seemed to be madly fussy and arrogant brutes—excepting always our own Chief—naturally drew us together, in the few odd moments when we weren't running or scrubbing madly and could shoot the breeze. There were some bullies, weaklings, loafers, and psychopaths, of course, but I found that most ordinary young American men, when shocked stiff by discipline and confinement, desperate for their women, living in a world wholly strange to them, and exhausted, were excellent company to be in in trouble, and even as wretched little boots they were somehow formidable. They could not be called civilized in any ordinary sense, but I thought they might well have no small hand in saving civilization. Most of them had clearly been tough and effective in their different hard jobs at home, and they were eager to learn to be sailors, "instead of all this shit," and to get on with the job. With less Momism than has been advertised, they were devoted to their families, and some few, in their ways, were truly religious. They had no "culture" at all, but some had a vague hungering for it. As citizens, they were ignorant and violently prejudiced, but I felt (or hoped) had a base of good sense and good will. When they were clearly stronger than I was, and more clever with their hands, they laughed at me affectionately and bore me a hand. I much preferred them to the class of new-rich, half-educated, "other-directed, status-seeking, organization men" and women. The clichés serve well enough.

Of course a boring amount of their talk was about sex, and their language was on the whole repetitious and dull, but some of this talk amused me. For example, I jotted down this scrap of conversation for Peggy: "So he got to playing with her titties, and she says, 'Mac, you like them titties, don't you? Well, they're all yours.' And by Jesus, she takes them off and hands them to him. They was all rubber! She didn't have no more titties than you or me. Boy, did we give *him* the bird!" I may say here that my memories of the sex life of the men I knew in the Navy, as I heard about it and observed it, fully support the Kinsey report, especially in its emphasis on the different levels of education. The sexual life of these men was crude in the extreme, and when they had to be and could be, even most of the married men were freely promiscuous, but at the same time their loyalty to their wives and their best girls was deep, and I suspected that most of them were or would be good husbands and fathers—warmer, more unselfish, more playful, and more firm in their own rights and dignity, than their bosses in civilian life.

From my first day in boot camp, when my turn came to stand naked in front of five officer-psychiatrists and one of them looked at my papers and said "My God, this man

is a *writer!*" I had to deal once more with the fact, caused
by my odd profession, my relatively superior education,
my language, my tastes, and my greater age, that I was an
odd-ball, an outsider. That first morning, when one of five
doctors at a table asked me baldly whether I was neurotic,
I said: "Certainly, Sir, but aren't we all?—ard in my
case it might be called an occupational disease." They
laughed, said I'd do all right, and without further questioning told me to get the hell out of there and on my way.
My basic rule, sufficiently obvious, was never either to
call attention to my peculiarities or to conceal them and
pretend to be anything different from what I was. Most
enlisted men found nothing very surprising or important in
the fact that while Joe Doakes puddled steel for a living
and liked to bowl, Charlie Smart wrote books and liked
to play squash. Many officers were more difficult in this
respect; I'll get to that later. During the war there were
probably more formally educated men in the ranks than
there are now, but as it happened I didn't meet very many
of them.

There is a related fact that I had to face, to my surprise,
and that is that among uneducated men, and even many
college men, a Harvard man is marked, is considered
something rather special or suspect. Maybe it's the accent,
maybe we are still (or were twenty years ago) all supposed
to be rich, and it may even be that more is expected of us.
It was at boot camp that I ran into this matter for the first
time in the Navy, when my good Chief kindly got me out
of my job of ordinary mess-cooking and into that of waiting on table in a Chiefs' mess. These Chiefs were a collection of pretty crude former athletes, and my Chief had
made the error of telling them that I was a Harvard man.
For a couple of days they kept taunting me and jeering at
me in various ways—especially, of course, about Harvard's

football teams. Soon I worked up an act: I turned myself into a supercilious "gentleman's gentleman." Taking care not to give anyone any real excuse for getting me into trouble, I kept a towel on my arm, waited on everyone very quickly and elaborately, hinted an English accent, and with a raised eyebrow, or an extra fork, or a faintly shocked "Sir?!" managed to convey the idea that I considered them all goons. Before I was taken off that job I had reduced the Chiefs at my table to mumbling silence while they shoveled in their food.

Another slight problem of this kind was that our good Chief kept trying to promote me to what is or was known as a "boot petty officer." These rating carried no extra pay or real authority, and seemed to me comparable to the different ratings in Boy Scouting. Besides, one of the things I had looked forward to in the Navy was the ease of not making any decisions or having to direct other people— at least until I knew very well what I was doing. However, I managed to talk myself out of most of these silly ratings.

Then I got a very high mark, for Great Lakes, on the general intelligence test, which did me no credit, and because of this and the fact that I had once worked in a merchant ship I was made a Seaman First, a true rating of sorts, with a little more pay. Although I still dodged being a "boot petty officer," I did coach lads as well as I could for some of the tests, especially in grammar, and when I was asked to, I enjoyed helping the boys write letters to their families and girls. The boys were chiefly nervous about spelling, and usually I did little more than clean that up, tighten the grammar, and remove a few clichés. Once, with the boy's commission and encouragement, I did write to his girl in Iowa, or somewhere, a long love letter that might have been written by Browning to his Ba. I never heard the result of that one. Meanwhile,

I had made a grade of 30 per cent in mechanical aptitude, which was no surprise to me, and finally was told that I'd be sent to a signal school.

At the end of our time in boot camp, we had a long period of waiting, wild scuttlebutt (gossip about our futures), hard mess-cooking, and depression. All this resulted in a number of fights, cases of insubordination, and absences over leave, all promptly punished. We were all eager to learn something, and to go aboard ships, but we *were* beginning to learn something—to wait indefinitely without too much hope or interest in the future, and to accept foul-ups as inevitable. It seems to me sensible to choose such things as one's work or one's wife with care, and to keep an eye open for the breaks, but whether it's Divinity or more immediately the Pentagon that shapes our ends, rough-hewing them seems to me a bit humorless and futile. The job's the thing, and enjoyment of the present. Perhaps because I need them, my favorite French words are *doucement, doucement, mon ami.*

5

After nearly two months in boot camp, I spent five months in the signal school at the University of Chicago.

In some respects, the conditions were much easier. We marched to and from classes, across a green campus, but we had very little drilling. We ate in a clubhouse or student union and had no mess-cooking, presumably because we were supposed to be spending our time studying. We had a good many liberties and were right in the city.

In other respects, it was rougher. Instead of decent barracks we had an old gymnasium on Stagg Field in which hundreds of us were packed like worms in a bait can, with three-tiered bunks close together, tiny lockers, and wholly inadequate facilities for keeping ourselves and our clothes clean, while the building itself could have been cleaned only by a good fire. Despite all the cleaning and painting details and all our real efforts to live decently, that place was an irremediable slum. Or rather it was an old-fashioned county jail or state penitentiary. We had the green football field for exercise, rest, and practice with hand flags, but it had our slum at one end, stands on one end and one side, and a high wall on the fourth side, its one gate complete with sentries.

This prison atmosphere was emphasized by the petty officers who pushed us around in our slum. These were not even Tunneyfish. God knows where the Navy had scraped them up, but none of them had ever been at sea, and one of our teachers, a wounded Signalman First from the regular Navy, told us that most of them had been guards in mental hospitals or would-be policemen. Our teachers included a few veterans like this one, but most of them were merely star graduates of this or other schools who had never walked a deck or previously taught a class. A few of the commissioned officers, whom we rarely saw except at parades and inspections, were good, but some of them were broken-down old reservists from World War I or very raw, young, and nervous Ensigns. Or so it seemed. We had all begun to lose our dazed timidity as boots and to ripen into regular convicts, toward whom the young Ensigns were properly nervous. We and they were saved from serious trouble only by the liberties, by the steady grind and mild interest of the work in classes, and by our ambition to get ratings and more money by being something other than useless boobs and boots if and when we were ever assigned to ships.

A few words about our "courses" are necessary. *Procedure* means all the methods of writing or translating messages so that they will be received by the proper ships for the proper responses at the right times. The language is highly formal and condensed, with some of the interest of a word game. Later we had to learn modifications of our procedure, for use with the British. I learned more procedure than I ever had to use, but of course some of us were going into major ships and complex situations of command. Semaphore with hand flags is of course very simple, as every Boy Scout knows, but it took me a long time to work up speed in reading and sending. *Flaghoist* is signaling by flags jerked from a "flag bag" (which is really a box) and run up on yardarms. It has its own procedure, which permits saying a great deal with very few flags, and it requires real alertness and some manual dexterity. We learned on masts set up in a field, which is much easier than working on the pitching and rolling bridges of ships far apart in foul weather or in a calm that leaves the flags hanging dead. *Blinker* is the sending and receiving of messages, by flashing lights, in Morse code. We learned it by spending hours daily in a huge, darkened field house, and here again I thought I'd never learn the damned stuff before my eyes gave out. There were evening classes for those who had flunked in the afternoon, and night after night I marched off with the other dullards.

Finally, to my great relief, all this penetrated my subconscious, so that I could listen and speak with flags and lights almost as easily and unconsciously as I could with my ears and mouth. I don't know why it took me and the others five whole months to learn these skills, which are relatively simple. It was clear enough that, as in learning languages, my age was a handicap, but the teen-agers weren't much faster. It may be that the psychologists, or more likely the neurologists, will find new and better ways of teaching and learning these and similar skills, which must have their counterparts in civilian life, outside of radio work and telegraphy. Perhaps they have already done so.

Another thing that interested me in this experience was the effectiveness, in teaching *this* kind of thing—though it would surely not work in other fields—of sheer force and repetition. The students didn't have the slightest interest in signaling as such, as a craft that had been devised in certain ways for certain purposes, and indeed there wasn't much to explore here at best—in marked contrast with quartermaster work and navigation. There was no attempt made to arouse any such interest. The teachers didn't know or care anything about teaching as a craft, and could easily have been replaced by machines. There were only the carrot of promotion and money, the stick of dirtier work with less money, and the ominpresent force of naval discipline. Like Horace Bixby, Mark Twain's master pilot, they were simply going to learn us or kill us, by God. And it worked. Ever since, I have been impatient with all the talk about motivating students, except very young ones, and with fancy, "permissive," and "democratic" methods, except for mature students of subjects involving values. A great deal can be beaten in, the lazy or unfit can or should be dropped, and the good minds will rebel and discover for themselves.

In that school, our rebellion against the slum housing and the broken-down cops dressed up like petty officers took the form of dodges, games, and pranks that were juvenile enough but that relieved our emotions and that provided some excitement because the rewards (an extra bounce in the hay or bottle of liquor, say) and the punishments (the brig and black marks on one's permanent record) were real enough. Our ringleader was a handsome boy, our section-leader, called Alabama, who got good marks and who cultivated the commissioned officers and also the sentries, boys who had been bilged out of school— all as cover for our operations. Once, for example, an Ensign discovered at evening muster the absence of a man Alabama had smuggled out for a last night with his wife, who had suddenly to go home to Nebraska or wherever. We successfully substituted another man who looked like the absentee and who hastily undressed and got into the showers, where he gave the absentee's name as his own and said he had not heard the call for muster. Through his substitute, of course, the absentee lost a liberty, but otherwise it would have been the brig and worse. Alabama finally landed in the brig himself, but not before he involved me in what might be called a foot-note to history.

Half of us were kept on duty every weekend, and when we had cleaned up the slum as well as we could, then cleaned it all over again, and done some painting, there were still long hours to kill. Then Alabama would fix it up with the sentries on the gate to allow one of us to go out in the whites required on liberty, with enough of our pooled money to buy several bottles of whiskey, and to return without questioning. On the weekend I did the illegal foraging, all went well until I was strolling back toward the gate, with my big brown paper parcel under my arm, in the company of a graduate student, a civilian, with whom I had got acquainted in a bar. Before we reached the gate, I noticed that the guard had been changed and that the sentry was staring at me suspiciously. I swung the civilian around and with him returned around the corner, out of sight of the sentry. We were then outside the western grandstand of Stagg Field. The area under the grandstand was walled tight, but there was one small door that I found unlocked. When I asked my companion if he knew where that door led to, he said, "Why yes, that goes to a metal-lurgical laboratory." (These very words I recorded at the time in a letter to Peggy.) I said good-by to him and went through the door. It was dim in there, but I saw structures under the stand, and more important to me, a GI can in which I could deposit my precious parcel for the time being, and also an opening onto the football field. There I lighted a cigarette and strolled across the field toward our slum. The sentry appeared from the gate and tried to question and seize me, but I talked fast and bewildered him, and when he went for an officer I disappeared into the slum, got out of my whites, and told my mates where the liquor could be found after dark. We had a quietly merry evening. I had to stand a watch beginning at midnight, and during it the good Signalman First I have mentioned chinned himself on my breath and asked me how the hell I got out for a drink. "Who? Me? *Out*?" I protested, then quickly changed to distracting talk about my problem with blinker. He certainly saw through my chatter, but he was a sailor and a mate, and he dropped it.

Years later I discovered what you will have guessed—that in that "metallurgical laboratory," quite unguarded, a group of brave geniuses were preparing in secrecy the first chain reaction in history, which was effected only a few weeks later. *Why* was that place unguarded? The only explanation I can imagine is that the authorities were acting on the principle of Poe's "Purloined Letter," and although I do not underestimate the authorities, I cannot quite believe this explanation.

Fortunately the comedy is often lighter, less resonant and disturbing. One evening an old friend of mine, Bill Crosby, a real sailor who happened at that time to be a Major in the Army, appeared and managed to spring me for a few hours from that jail. He appeared in a shiny car driven by an Army Captain, whom I saluted smartly when I was introduced, before I climbed into the back of the car with the Major. My friend and I tied one on, but he was careful to deliver me back to my jail just on time. All the sentries snapped to attention for him while I told them grandly to "Carry on, son!" Then I went inside and played Tarzan, as we called it, swinging from bar to bar of the tiered bunks and awakening everyone nearby. It is a curious fact that although during my years as an enlisted man I could easily and perhaps sometimes should have been roughed up, physically or at least verbally, more than once, I was not once touched or insulted, except in obvious play and good nature.

Late in October, as this phase of schooling for our "class" drew near its end, there occurred again the general tightening up of the jail, with more mugging and finger-printing, the cancellation of liberties and leaves, the flood of scuttlebutt about our futures, and the increase of tensions. At this time that same good Signalman First, named Kinney, gave me an offer, not an order, from the officers, to remain at the school indefinitely as an instructor. If I accepted, I'd be made a Signalman Third, and if I declined, I'd be sent to sea without that rating, as a signalman's striker, or apprentice. I was not ordered to stay at the school because they preferred volunteers, if they could get any who were good enough and yet not suspiciously eager to stay ashore. The proffered rating was a bribe of sorts, with a sting if declined, because anyone good enough as a signalman to be a teacher was clearly good enough to be sent to sea with a rating, as others not desired as teachers would be. This struck me as comically unfair but not important. I wanted to go to sea, where I figured I could earn a rating soon enough, so I declined the offer with thanks. Once by semaphore across Stagg Field, that old sailor asked me to reconsider, and when, with all the speed with those flags I could manage, I again declined, he signaled "You'll be sorry; that's the mistake of the year." This scared me a little, because I didn't want to be rough-hewing my way to Davy Jones' locker.

After a rather silly graduation ceremony, with no rating for Smart, I had a harrowingly emotional week at home and then was shipped off to the East Coast.

6

As long as anyone is in the Navy, they keep sending him back to school, to different camps, bases, and training ships. That first winter and each of the following two, between ships I spent about two months in various amphibious training bases in or near Norfolk, Virginia, or on Chesapeake Bay, and in LSTs used for training on the Bay itself. That first winter, I found most of the many different kinds of training fascinating in themselves, as later I was to find them very useful.

Otherwise, the life in those training bases and ships almost all of us, I think, found endlessly irritating and depressing. The barracks, bunks, and chow were good, and by this time all of us were more or less used to the endless clothes-washing, work details, watch-standing, and all that, so necessary to keep men clean and out of trouble. Many more of the petty and commissioned officers in charge had been at sea than had been the case early in the war in and around Chicago, but the morale in any training base or ship is bound, I suspect, to be bad, for many reasons. The commissioned and petty officers in charge are apt to be there either against their will; because of age, wounds, accidents, errors, or arbitrary decrees from on high; or, in far fewer cases, because they have managed somehow to wangle those slots in order to stay ashore in greater comfort and safety, near their wives or doxies.

The former group are bitter, and the latter are nervous. All of them are tense and rough, because to a certain degree they have to be. They have on their hands a constantly changing mass of trainees, whom they can never know personally, who don't know each other, who cannot be expected to have any loyalty toward the base and its job, such as most sailors feel toward their ship and her company, and who are near enough to their women and cities to want liberty all the time. Most of them have been in the Navy long enough to know all the tricks of getting out of work and making life difficult for their superiors. I suspect that all those camps and ships were and are close enough to Washington to have plenty of higher officers inspecting them and bearing down hard, all the time. All the trainees and most of the officers in charge want only to get through the tour somehow and back aboard a ship of their own. For me and the other trainees in those winters the gloom was deepened by the cold, the darkness, and the grimness of the surroundings. Even on the North Atlantic, I have never been so cold, without proper clothing, as I have been on Chesapeake Bay. Washington and Baltimore are fine, in their ways, if you can get there, but Norfolk has had too much of the Navy too long, and has responded by becoming, in the view of all sailors, the Ass-Hole of the Universe.

The first time, however, it was a sheer delight to smell salt water at last, to watch the gulls foraging, and to see the great and little fighting ships in the yards. Some of us sneaked aboard HMS *Queen Elizabeth,* an ancient and honorable veteran of even the Dardanelles and Zeebrugge, that in our war had been mined and shot up and was a mess; and then aboard the *Alabama,* brand-new and about to go to sea. For all her weight of guns and armor, the latter seemed as beautiful to us as a clipper ship. Standing in awe on her signal bridge, which we were told had a crew of forty men, we discovered with relief and some pride that we could read a discussion between two other ships by blinker about the exact time of sunset. At a recreation center, we shot the breeze with some American sailors who had been on the Murmansk run and with some limeys who had made three trips to Dunkirk and, in a trawler, had chased the Nazi ships up the Channel when they escaped from Brest. We weren't sailors yet and we felt it keenly, but at least we were in good company.

First we were hauled by truck to a "fire-fighting school" down on a beach somewhere. The instruction was concrete, practical, fast, and clear, by men who had been firemen as civilians. Lectures were alternated with demonstrations outdoors. They had a steel-and-concrete structure built like the innards of a destroyer, and we learned how to crawl around on the decks under smoke. In this mock-up and in tanks, they would set off big oil and gasoline fires, and then put them out, letting us take part whenever possible. They used water with different nozzles, steam, foam, CO_2, and other tricks. There were also demonstrations of gas masks and a diving helmet. Here it was, I think, that we saw for the first time a movie called *The School of the Firefighter*, which we were to see hundreds of times later like those on venereal disease, but probably not too often.

On other days we were taken to another beach for training on the 20-mm. antiaircraft guns that were the chief weapons in LSTs at that time. These had magazines of sixty shells about nine inches long, and it took three men to handle and fire each gun. Every other shell was a tracer, so the man strapped to the gun and firing it used it like a hose, leading the target, which was a sleeve towed by a plane off the beach. I was fairly good at this, perhaps because of my duck-shooting, but when it came to taking the gun apart, cleaning it, and putting it back together, which we did again and again, I always had a mad struggle, and was liberally cursed by the Chief Gunner's Mate who taught us. I always seemed to find some damned part of the gun left over!

Meanwhile, at our home base near Norfolk, signal drills continued, and we had further lessons in first aid, gas masks, and other matters of importance, mixed with setting-up exercises and even softball games. Finally—and it *was* finally, because we were always restless to get on with it—we were taken to a camp near Solomons Branch, Maryland, on a little peninsula of mud in the Bay. Here, besides the inevitable routines, we were actually assigned to a crew, with mates who seemed promising, and with nervous young officers whom we eyed with interest. Each of us had a "slot," and mine, as a mere Seaman First, signalman's striker, was implausibly that of "Acting Chief Quartermaster." A quartermaster is, besides a signalman, an enlisted assistant to a navigator.

On my thirty-eighth birthday, which I kept strictly to myself, I received a handsome present. Along with a pleasant and intelligent young signalman from our crew, Howard E. Gembler, and a few other enlisted men from other crews, I was put in a course in navigation, primarily for officers. With sessions morning, afternoon, and evening, it would last only a few days, but at least it would be a start. For six months I had had no truly intellectual exercise, and from the very beginning navigation proved to be a delight of that nature, a relief from hard physical work and rough personal relations (however valued), and a challenge to learn how to do something on which the lives of ships and men depended. The parts of a 20-mm. gun, or even a .45 pistol, would evidently always leave me baffled and helpless; anchors, winches, bow-door machinery, and all that I finally knew something about, if never enough; and the great diesel engines always remained to me a total mystery; but navigation, I felt at once, was something in which I might eventually earn the right to be dressed up like a sailor. At Harvard I had taken a short course in astronomy, and although I had forgotten almost all of it, I found that it did help me to learn again such things as the different kinds of time. Anyone at all curious about this craft and the superb data and instruments that make it possible can glance into the classic books by Bowditch and Dutton, which we used steadily at sea, or into the excellent *Introduction* by Messrs. Shute, Shirk, Porter, and Hemenway, four former colleagues of mine at Choate. I had had little mathematics, so like most of the others, I had to rely on the short cuts through trigonometry: H.O. 211 and H.O. 214, and it was only years later, for fun, that I taught myself how to solve spherical triangles. Perhaps the most useful thing I learned at college was not to be afraid of unfamiliar kinds of knowledge.

One of the delights of this very short course was our teacher, a Lieutenant Strong, who I think had taught astronomy at the University of California. One night he explained the interesting arcs of lines of position—a central idea, and not an easy one—with a huge diagram drawn on the board by himself, as good a job of teaching as I had seen for years. Then he dismissed the officers, kept us enlisted men, and treating us as gentlemen and his equals, as he always did, he gave us a little lecture on how to get along with our navigating officers. It was a very shrewd and humane performance. He said that the younger officers would not know much more about navigation or anything else than we did, but that our skippers would. Of the younger officers he said, "Always say 'Aye, aye,

Sir!' and bear a hand sharply and cheerfully, as though they were old salts. It will make them feel good, and God knows they will have to have something or someone to make them feel good. Take me for example. I can take a ship anywhere, but I'm not sure I could always keep you in underwear and coffee." And so on, returning us that night, briefly, to civilization. Two years later, in the same place, I ran across this excellent teacher bossing the maintenance crew of the camp!

This running into old shipmates was one of the small delights of naval life. For example, at the signal school I had found a buddy, only somewhat younger than myself, if baldheaded, named Bob Schrader. He was a "gentleman" but I called him "the bald-pated satyr." He appeared at Norfolk, and again at Solomons, and although he was there assigned to an LCI, I was to run into him several times in the Pacific. He had a fiancée somewhere not too far from us there on the East Coast, and he was always figuring how he could reach her college town by bus. Once when we were going somewhere in a truck, he asked the driver about this, and the driver said, "What cooks? You got a piece of cunt down there?" Deadpan, Schrader replied, "Yes, she's the Assistant Dean of Women at Blank University."

A couple of bitterly cold weeks in December, we spent aboard a training LST, with her own ship's company, and with two other training crews, barging up and down Chesapeake Bay. Many photographs have made the general appearance and structure of the LSTs sufficiently familiar. At first we were disappointed to be assigned to these "barges," which looked at first so ugly and were indeed so slow (about twelve knots flank, nine cruising), but after a while many of us felt a certain amount of affection for them and pride in them, and in ourselves.

It became apparent that the war was going to be won, if ever, by armies transported great distances and put ashore on beaches usually defended, and that actually the great battleships, carriers, destroyers, submarines, and all the rest were slugging it out with each other chiefly in order to protect or destroy our passengers and ourselves. Sir Winston Churchill wrote that he and all the top commanders were counting the LSTs like jewels. In the large family of landing craft, the LSTs were more comfortable and independent than the smaller vessels and not so impersonal and dull as the transports. It was early apparent that if we were bungling little tramps as sailors, both the Navy and the Army would have been helpless without us. The LSTs had no keels and so yawed madly, but they had a high metacentric height, and although we had plenty of groundings and rammings, the fact is that not one LST was lost except as a result of enemy action. In short, these ships and her men delivered the goods, if I do say so, and some day the Naval Institute will get around to publishing our story.

On that training cruise, of course, we were all worms and slaves, made to do all the dirty work and pushed out of the way when anything interesting was to be done, but in a ship even this was better than in any camp. The constant drills of all kinds—general quarters, fire, special sea detail, and all the rest—were dull but instructive; and of course Gembler and I were fascinated by the signals and by whatever we were allowed to see of the gyro and magnetic compasses, the peloruses, the lead line, the chronometers, the sextants, the charts, and the rest of the navigational gear, all *in use*. I found that I could remember a fair amount of all this, and about the buoys and lights, from my summer at sea eighteen years before, and we had Navy books to study. I also found that I could still take bearings and handle the wheel under orders. Of course all our mates in our crew, in the other divisions, were also beginning to learn their crafts in actual use. Frank Woodall, our own good head cook, working with the ship's cooks, made some bread, and when I asked him how it turned out, he laughed and said, "Charlie, it was lousy; it squatted to rise, and it baked on the squat."

Christmas was approaching, and of course we all wondered where we'd be, whether we'd get any liberty, and whether we could reach our women or they us. Anything like that seemed too lucky to happen, and then it did happen; we headed for Baltimore! On the way into that port, the ship's arrogant officers were taken down a peg when they ran her aground in a fog, near a lighthouse, but managed to get her off. We were warned severely not to say a word about this accident, but as soon as some of us got ashore and into a cab, the driver said, "I hear you boys had some trouble down there by the light."

Somehow I managed to get word to Peggy and she managed to reach Baltimore. She had been very happy there as a girl, and after the few hours we had together in that old city, I loved it as much as she did. In addition, we had a few hours together in Washington, mostly at a dinner party at the home of Peggy's awesome uncle and aunt, Mr. and Mrs. Charles Warren. Entering late in my gob suit, once again I felt shy in such company, but Uncle Charles rose from the table, gripped my hand, and said to his guests, "And now here's a *real* sailor!" I only wished I was. Aunt Nancy inadvertently gave me a naval officer's necktie, and on leaving, I cached it behind a mirror in the lower hall, where months later it was recovered by Peggy's brother, a Lieutenant.

The next day, this "real sailor" had to "run up the mast" to clear the commission pennant at the truck, and did not

succeed in doing so because he came near to freezing from
vertigo! We had another week aboard, and then went back
to the old round at Norfolk, where the scuttlebutt seethed.
Meanwhile, we were getting acquainted with more of our
mates and officers. On the bridge with us, Gembler and I
had Freddy Medeiros, a good but somber Portuguese lad
with a mouth organ, and a bouncy, delightful radioman
named "Ginny" Giannatasio. There was also a tough and
witty motor mac named Ralph Davis. These and others
seemed the kind of men with whom one could share a raft,
and months later, on the other side of the world, I had not
changed my mind. Our Communications Officer was a
friendly, sensitive young man named Mr. Carlson; the
Executive Officer and navigator was a tense young man
named Mr. Meddaugh who had just returned from rough
times on the African coast near Casablanca; and the
Captain, Lieutenant Perdue, was a dry, competent-look-
ing former quartermaster in the regular Navy, perhaps
my age or a little older. We and they could only hope for
the best. Early in January 1943, with four other crews, we
boarded a train for Oregon to get, at long last, our own
ship.

7

That was a weird five-day trip, and those crowded cars should have been drawn by Hogarth, Pascin, or Pop Hart. We were in old Pullmans of sorts, of course without porters, and with a few much-harassed conductors and trainmen. Bunks came up or down as we pleased, night or day, laundry was hanging all over the place, everyone seemed to be singing, yelling, or snoring, and the total effect was that of a cheerful slum. We had a dining car or two, but we had to stand in line for hours, yelling and cursing, to get any food at odd hours of the day or night. The Navy had its share of dirty little squirts, and on that train, as in perhaps a very few of the crews' quarters in the ships, they set the tone.

In the rare, more quiet corners and odd moments, I got acquainted with a few more of my own good shipmates, including notably Lloyd Shelton, already and justly a Boatswain's Mate First Class. He was a huge, powerful man, so that nobody ever gave him any lip, but he was very gentle. He was twenty-eight years old, a fisherman by trade who had fished for porgies (used for oil and chicken feed) all up and down the East Coast, but his home was somewhere on Chesapeake Bay. He had been married for seven years, and his wife was at that time paralyzed. He knew nothing at all about the Navy, but he obviously knew a great deal about the sea, ships, boats, and all their gear, and we were all happy to think that he would be in our ship.

On our first morning out, on the C & O, we went right through the gravel plant where I had heard about Pearl Harbor, and then the train swung around Mount Logan and gave us a clear view of my home town and our own hills, all lightly dusted with snow. It shook me, and I was glad that Peggy was at that time in Massachusetts. Once out in the Dakotas somewhere, a boy who had been staring out of a window eagerly for hours, suddenly beat his fist on the glass and cried, "Jesus *Christ!* There's our place . . . and there's my *dog!*" Someone unearthed a concealed remnant of his own liquor, bought during a brief stop in St. Paul, and let this lad knock himself out with it.

At 0230 one morning we sacked in at the Naval Receiving Station, somewhere outside Portland, on the Willamette River. This was a good, small station, clean and comfortable, with only a few hundred amphibious sailors in it at a time—half of them in the British and Canadian navies. The weather itself was oddly English, with fine rain, quickly changing sun and clouds, usually almost balmy, with sudden changes to a nip in the air or to real cold, with snow. More inoculations, and more colds and fevers. Once when I was in sick bay next to me was an old English Chief with pneumonia, and delirious. He was a tough old nut, but he kept moaning and saying, "Dearie-me-oh-my-oh! What a to-do, my pretty one!" She was probably a nice, fat old biddy type in London, under the bombs, and I hoped that she could feel her old man's love across a continent and an ocean.

For several days and nights I had to stand the quartermaster's watch, from 0000 to 0400 and from 1200 to 1600. On that base, this meant holding down the desk and telephone outside the executive office and checking all men and vehicles in and out. I was madly busy with matters about which I knew almost nothing, and could only guess and improvise. Once the Officer of the Day dashed in to say that he had a *women's* committee outside, from Portland, who had somehow got the authority to inspect the canteen: send my messenger up there on the double and get the contraceptives to hell out of sight off the counter. "Sir," asked the messenger, "do you mean the rubbers?" On their way out, the ladies kindly presented the quartermaster's office with an electric coffee pot, for which I was told to write them a note of thanks at once.

After that, Freddy Medeiros and I had to teach signals to a gang who knew even less about them than we did, but we also wormed our way into a class in marlinespike seamanship given by our own Boats, Shelton. Presently Gembler, Medeiros, and I were joined, in our own bridge gang, by an actual Quartermaster Third named Kenneth Silvester, or Silver, who did not resent my being slotted above him, and who turned out to be a good signalman and quartermaster and an excellent shipmate. The boys on the bridge are apt to be good, and some would say they are apt to know it. In my eagerness to spend less time teaching signals and more time learning other things, I got into trouble with a warrant officer, who put me on night watches with a rifle and bayonet on a pier that was icy cold and infested with huge rats. One night on my pier there appeared to me the ghostly figure of a seventy-two-year-old elevator man, a Norwegian, who talked to me about the endless days in summer near Trondheim, the odors of the forest and the sea in spring, and the long silence of his brother and sister still living there—he hoped. "For this relief, much thanks. . . ."

In those days and nights I was indeed sick at heart, because I heard about a disaster in our family, a severe mental illness that was brutal for all concerned and that poisoned the relations between us for years. The worst experience for any man in the armed forces is to get bad news from home when he cannot do anything about it. The wife of one of my shipmates, who loved her dearly, ran off with his own brother. I heard of one boy, in another ship, who passed out cigars to celebrate the birth of a son. His shipmates were struck dumb, a rare occurrence in the Navy, and then violent, suppressed arguments broke out, about a moral problem; should they tell the poor little fool or not? Finally, to stop fights, the Captain himself had to intervene and remind the poor boy that he had not been near his wife for much more than a year.

Although Portland was considerably upset by the influx of servicemen and shipbuilders, it was an excellent liberty town, full of generous and imaginative people. Wellesley friends of my sister's entertained me and a mate like princes, and I spent happy hours reading and writing in the George A. White Service Men's Center. It was there that I was able to make and send to Peggy a disc of passages from The Song of Songs, which is Solomon's. If I had not been reading from the Bible about "the Church's love unto Christ," I am sure that the nice lady operating the machine would have felt forced to object to this unequalled example of erotic poetry.

In one way or place or another, throughout the war, I managed to find a good many books, and reading was one of my salvations. The three volumes that I carried everywhere in my seabag were the Nonesuch selection of Hazlitt's essays, a compact Oxford Shakespeare, and Isak Dinesen's *Seven Gothic Tales*. These were escape hatches that I found more reliable than the Perry Mason tales that served my mates so well, but they were more than escape; they seemed more "real" and revealing than more "realis-

tic" works of all kinds; they were better guides to the implausible world in which I lived, in which we all live. As
a part of his gusto and sense of wonder, Hazlitt loved
paintings much as I did, and Peggy kept sending me post-
cards from museums. In my low moments, I could get
from a battered postcard of a painting by Vermeer something very important to me.

We were all becoming very impatient to get our own
ship, which was being built with others in the Kaiser shipyard in Vancouver, Washington, a small city on the Columbia River a few miles from Portland. One day our
Supply Officer, Ensign Arra J. Kechijian, took his gentle-
manly storekeeper, Harvey L. Potter, and me up to the
shipyard to help him check the stores for our fat old lady,
whose number was 456. Mr. Kechijian was, I think,
Armenian in origin, a tough, cheerful, and competent little
man who had been in the dry-cleaning business in Provi-
dence. The quantity and variety of our stores seemed to me
fantastic. When we finally got aboard, we were fascinated
by the men and women working on her, as they evidently
were by us. Their high wages troubled me for hours, because Peggy was at that time hard-pressed for money, and
I wondered whether I had been a selfish fool to enlist instead of getting a job like these. However, when one man
said to me as we left, "Well! good luck, sailor, you can
have my share of this fucking tub" I said, "Thanks, I'll
take it." What I felt like adding was, "Step aside, please,
ladies and gentlemen. It's our turn now. We are going to
take this fucking tub to her job."

On another morning, eleven of us enlisted men were
turned out very early and taken to our ship for a trial run.
Included were Boats and Gene Cote, our senior motor
machinist's mate. Cote was a garage-owner with a wife
and several children, whom he missed as sorely as I missed

my wife. He was tops at his job, tough but gentle, dryly humorous, and wholly adult. On board we found the Captain; the First Lieutenant, Mr. Malloy; the Engineering Officer, Mr. Martin; an old river pilot, a merchant captain, a representative of the Maritime Commission, and several inspecting naval officers not in our ship's company. Several of our own officers were still at school elsewhere. When we went aboard, the sun was just rising, magenta, above a mountain range, and this colored light on the water, plus the reflected lights of the shipyard, made a scene more theatrical than natural. We had various speed trials, and tests of all the deck and steering gear. Several of us from our bridge gang had half-hour tricks at the wheel. All the gear seemed to be in good order— what an illusion that turned out to be! There were many civilians on board, including six or eight women in the galley who, to our astonishment, served us lunch with tablecloths, fresh fruit, and free cigarettes.

That was the end of pampering, because the next few days we spent moving and stowing the stores and ammunition. This job, for all hands, was a killer, and we were all at it for hours on end whenever we were in any port and often at sea. Often I thought I'd drop to the deck or down a ladder, and if I had not just had eight years of farming, I probably could not have taken it. On February 3, 1943, USS *LST 456* was put in commission in a short ceremony on the fantail, and somehow Silvester, Gembler, Medeiros, and I got the commission pennant up on the truck, the ensign up on the stern, and the jack on the jackstaff in the bow, simultaneously, at the right moment. That old quartermaster, our Captain, was properly fussy about all such matters. Then with the pilot we took her to my old pier in Portland, where we stayed for several days, getting final stores, stowing them, and trying to get our different departments organized. Our officers were of course nervous and irritable, and we were frequently interrupted by visiting officers who came aboard to make inspections and give final little lessons about this and that.

Eventually we got under way, still of course with a river pilot, and started down the Willamette and Columbia rivers for Astoria, Oregon, about seventy-five miles from Portland. Now began some trouble that aged the Captain (and incidentally myself) appreciably and that brought some dreadful curses, deserved or not, down on the heads of one Henry J. Kaiser and his minions.

Once when I was at the helm, getting orders from the pilot on the coning tower a deck above me, I was ordered to "come right a little" to dodge the pier of a bridge. When I turned the wheel, there was no response whatever, and my heart nearly stopped dead. I shouted up the tube, "Sir, the steering gear has gone!" Both the pilot and the Captain came rushing down to the wheelhouse, made a quick test of the wheel themselves, and just in time, steered the ship with the two engines.

Every electrician on board got on that job, and they fixed the control box in the steering-gear compartment, below decks and aft, but only temporarily. They claimed that much of the electrical steering gear was used material. Every few hours that damned gear would fail, and the Captain nearly had a stroke. Somewhere—probably on that training cruise—I had learned how to take several men below and rig for steering with hand windlasses down there, while getting orders from the bridge by phone, but that was hard work, and more important, not very safe in a river. When we reached Astoria, the Captain fetched aboard some presumed experts, who worked on our steering gear for several hours, then reported that it was all in order. We had hardly started down the river when the infernal gear went out again. The Captain took her right back to the pier and went ashore for the experts, with a flush on his face that boded them no good. More repairs, and another report that all was in order.

The next morning, February 13, we got under way again, and I had the helm for four and a half hours, never knowing when that gear would fail. We moved into a spectacular sunset, and at the mouth of the river were met by a boat to take off the pilot. As the light failed and the moon and stars came out, we sighted the little merchant ship, the *Idaho,* that was waiting to be our company to San Diego, but of course both she and our ship were darkened. I never did find out why we were traveling with that merchant ship. Perhaps it was because we were known to have defective steering gear. Perhaps it was because, of the forty-six enlisted men and seven officers aboard, only five of us, I think—the Captain, the Exec, Boats, a coxswain from Gloucester, Massachusetts, and myself—had ever been more than a mile offshore. Perhaps not many men aboard were exhilarated, as I was, to feel that new ship, for the first time in her life, begin slowly to rise and then fall. We had a long way to go, but finally we were on our way.

8

In these days it may be necessary to remark that life in a naval vessel at sea bears almost no resemblance to that in a passenger ship on a pleasure cruise. The Captain of an LST had a cabin and head of his own, as befitted his quasi-divinity, while the other officers were bunked two or three in a stateroom, with any other officers who were passengers. At that time the crew lived in one compartment aft, about fifty feet square, with the bunks three deep, and when there were passengers, soldiers and marines going to work, they had compartments running fore and aft beside and above the tank deck. After the Japs had cleverly dropped bombs into several crews' quarters, the ships' companies were mixed with the passengers, so that most of the sailors operating a ship would be less apt to be killed at once, paralyzing the ship. We all had to spend much of our free time keeping our bunks and quarters clean and neat and washing our clothes, usually in buckets of salt water. We wore blue dungarees, blue cotton shirts, white hats, and heavy shoes, while the officers wore khaki chinos. The food, medical care by corpsmen, and (no less important) mail service, were usually very good, and in general we lived and worked in much greater comfort than the soldiers and marines, and than had been known by any other sailors, naval or merchant, in history.

Usually we stood watches, doing our own special kinds

of work, four hours on and eight off; on the bridge the
morning and evening watches, with dawn and sunset, and
with breaks for chow, were much the best. In combat zones
we stood watches four hours on and four off; and of course
before, during, and after attacks on the beaches, all hands
were on their feet all the time—up to seventy-two hours
straight or more, until they dropped. This does not mean
that we usually worked eight hours a day, or a mere fifty-
six hours a week. Although at least a third of the officers
and men were working at night under way and a good
many in port, during the days there was little time for
clothes-washing, sleeping, reading, writing letters, and so
on even when one was not on watch. The maintenance
work was endless, several different drills for all hands were
held daily, and in combat zones we were at general quarters for an hour or two or three every dawn and dusk. My
guess is that we averaged ninety or a hundred hours of
work, and forty hours of sleep, per week—which was all
right for efficiency and even for morale, except for the lack
of sleep, and I don't see how that could have been helped.
In war there seems to be time only for the Big Sleep.

My own work on the bridge I found increasingly interesting. Besides standing my own regular watches as a
signalman and quartermaster, I was, it now appeared, a
sort of secretary and factotum to any officers working on
the bridge. At any time I had to know where any instru-
ment, document, or flag was, and to have ready or figure
out quickly on demand such data as times of sunrise and
sunset, the location of stars and planets, the characteristics
of lights and other navigational aids, the conditions of tides
and currents, and so on. There was also the endless job of
correcting the charts from *Notices to Mariners*. I was often
given the wheel on tricky occasions, and on most of the
drills I was Captain's talker, receiving the reports and

transmitting the orders by sound-powered phones on the conning tower. "My" boys were reliable and congenial, and they accepted my somewhat Pickwickian authority admirably.

With the officers other than the Captain, my relations were more complex and difficult. It was partly the old problem of my being older, better educated, and even in some respects more experienced than they were, while they necessarily had much more authority and responsibility, and a few privileges. There had to be that gulf between us, with no room for friendship or any conflict of loyalties. This situation embarrassed them more than it did me or the Captain, but the demands of our work shoved it aside, and humor lubricated it.

Beneath all this, what chiefly wore down and embittered the morale of all the officers and men in each of the three ships in which I served, and probably in most of the other ships in the new Navy, was our anxiety about the obvious ignorance and incompetence of ourselves, our superiors, and our inferiors, while we lived very closely together for long periods in some danger, under the immense pressures of the Navy and of our desire to do as well as we could. In 456 this anxiety made the young officers sarcastic or a bit hysterical, and the men—often older and of proved merit ashore—bitterly contemptuous and resentful, while the Captain, although a real sailor with a merry glint in his eye, was worn down by sheer fatigue. In a Navy expanded as rapidly as ours had to be, I don't see how this situation could have been avoided; nevertheless, the job was done. For my part, I learned too slowly and never completely to escape from this miasma of distrust and bitterness into my own interesting jobs, the beauty and wonder of the sea, and the comradeship that so often came my way, warming my entrails.

In the crew's quarters of *456,* despite this anxiety and resentment, despite the constant taunting in very rough language, and despite the outbursts of savage anger between men living too closely together under great pressures, comradeship and decency were dominant. It is very hard to say surely what makes one crew more efficient and happy than another. In that ship, we were all volunteers fairly early in the war, and a common phrase was "Well, we asked for it!" Unlike some of the officers, we all respected and trusted that old mustang, the Captain. There is much in the luck of the draw, and we had many strong, competent, and decent men like Boats Shelton, Gene Cote, Santarcangelo the shipfitter, Jack Donovan, and others who were leading petty officers or born leaders, or both, and somehow these men set the tone. We also had our share of delightful eccentrics, such as Ralph Davis, always bitching, but the man who much later heaved a dud bomb overboard; and Floyd Bosler, the ship's clown, from Kansas City, *Kansas* (as he always insisted), who said once: "I sure don't know what the hell I'm doing in this tub, with all you ill-bred by-blows, boors, and roughnecks. Me, I was raised gently, for much better company, and for 'gracious living,' including a little sleep from time to time. I should have stayed right there on Sandusky Street and been a fucking air-raid warden."

In odd moments, I'd find myself on the fantail with two or three of these men, each of us with a mug of coffee in his hand, watching the clouds, the waves, and the wake, talking shop, bitching about the poor little ninety-day wonders, taunting Bosler into a comeback, reminiscing about our homes and old jobs, and guessing about the future. Except for some friendly curiosity and wonder, none of these men gave a damn about my peculiar background. We all took the same shit from above and felt silently that if we had to die, we couldn't want any better company. Somehow I have always been an outsider, but I have never felt less so than I did in the crew of that ship.

Peggy had given me a folder for letter paper, and in it I kept snapshots of her and of our house. We all had such pictures and showed them among friends, and one boy said of Peggy, "She looks intellectual and nice. I like them with a pug-nose." I think it was Ralph Davis who stared at the picture of our house and produced a conversation something like this:

"Jesus H. *Christ,* Charlie, are you *rich?*"

"Hell, no!"

"Then how do you keep up that fucking mansion?"

"God knows. My great-grandfather built it, and since then, none of us has had that kind of money."

And then, with a grin and a friendly tap of a huge fist on my chin, "I always figgered you was a fucking aristocrat."

"Well, hardly. I write for money, and my shit smells."

"And you know it, Charlie; you know it."

9

On that first voyage down the West Coast, we were in sight of land fairly often, and the sun rose gloriously from behind the coastal mountains. The sea was bright blue on clear days, and we saw sea lions and porpoises at play, while it amused us to discover that gulls could actually pick and scratch at their lice while gliding in the air and sideslip only a little. Several times we were buzzed by fast Navy planes, while we fumbled with the recognition signals and wondered whether we could get the guns going against Japs moving that fast. There was more trouble with the steering gear, but the electricians managed to keep us going without using the hand steering gear, and they kept up this successful tinkering for several weeks until we could get a real overhaul. One night we ran into a moderate gale, and rough weather was always hard on the boys in the galley. Many of the men were wretchedly seasick, as I have never been, thank God. Most of them recovered soon enough, but for months afterward a few poor devils were wretched every time we felt more than a very slight roll and pitch.

Just at dusk, the evening before we reached San Diego and long after the merchant ship had left us, a formation of ships appeared off our starboard bow; three battleships and five destroyers, all moving at what seemed to us great speed. Every man not standing a watch below appeared

on the weather deck, and the Captain relieved the OD. I
was standing watch at the blinker searchlight, and I had to
swallow my heart when the first battleship began talking
to us by blinker. I think he kept repeating *OE, OE, OE.* I
didn't have the dimmest notion what that meant, and
neither did Mr. Carlson or the Captain, who was, shall I
say, annoyed with both of us. Finally the Admiral, or who-
ever he was, also became annoyed with us, and said right
out in plain Samuel F. B. Morse: "What kind of a ship
are you?"

"Tell him, *tell* him," said the Captain, laughing grimly,
and with the proper procedure, I batted out as fast as I
could "Landing Ship Tank."

Then the Admiral told us to stay clear, and that impressive array went aft of us about its business, but presently a
destroyer came dashing back to us and repeated the warning. Evidently the Admiral had begun to doubt that we
farmers in the new Navy had understood him. Later, far
astern of us, the big boys began firing tracer shells in practice, and it was interesting how slowly they seemed to arc
through the darkness, just as from a distance the water in
a fall seems to drop slowly. The next day Mr. Carlson got
the latest signals from a shore office and we discovered that
OE turned out to be the way of asking a *merchant* ship its
identity. The Admirals and the world know better now.

One night in San Diego I got liberty until 0600 the next
morning, and I caught a bus to Encinitas, where Peggy's
brother, Rod Hussey, a Lieutenant, was serving as Exec of
the boat basin at Camp Pendleton and living with his wife
and two small sons. The Husseys were out, and the baby-
sitter properly didn't allow the sailor in until one of the
boys, Christopher, cried "Unc!" The parents did not return
until midnight, and then we sat up talking and drinking
until three or four. The alarm clock failed us, and facing

my first AOL, I insisted that the Lieutenant return with me to San Diego, come aboard, and get me out of trouble. He readily agreed, and said that we'd take Christopher, then about seven years old, with us in his car. On the dock in San Diego, we luckily met the boat from *456,* which had brought a church party ashore. When we came alongside the ship, there arose the problem of getting small Christopher safely up the Jacob's ladder. Boats passed down a line, and I secured this around Christopher's chest. He then rode on my shoulders as I climbed the ladder. When we reached the deck, Christopher saw his father and me salute the ensign and the OD, Mr. Carlson, and he solemnly imitated us. Mr. Carlson courteously escorted the Lieutenant to the wardroom, while I took Christopher aft to the galley and then the crew's quarters. We were late for chow, but Frank Woodall gave us both pancakes. While we were eating in crew's quarters, we were surrounded by men grinning nostalgically at the small boy and talking to him. Many of these men had children at home. Christopher was rather overcome, especially when huge Boats sat down beside him and said, "Christopher, don't you want to go with us across the Pacific? We need a cabin boy, and I just figure we'll take you along with us." On leaving the ship, after saluting again, Christopher insisted on climbing down the ladder by himself—but of course he was insured by that line. After they had gone, Mr. Meddaugh ate me out, but I gathered that the Lieutenant's talk with the Captain had saved me from Captain's Mast.

There is a better way to get out of jams like that. We took the ship to San Pedro for degaussing, and after that was done, to test its effectiveness, we ran her back and forth above sunken instruments. I was on the wheel and one of the engines failed, but I steered her well enough so that the Navy pilot complimented the Captain, who mut-

tered mysteriously in reply, "Hell, he ought to be good."
Not long after that, I got a "crow," wheel, and one stripe
on my right arm, as Quartermaster Third Class. Years
later, I heard Air Chief Marshall Sir Guy Garrod startle a
faculty and delight a few of them by saying that for professional airmen he preferred former students of the Greek
and Roman classics. Maybe Shakespeare and Hazlitt will
do.

When we returned to San Diego, we went outside the
harbor somewhere, to a sandy beach full of people, for
training in beaching the ship. This is a tricky operation,
which none of our officers had ever directed. In charge,
therefore, was a visiting Lieutenant Commander, complete
with fruit salad on his chest and a very superior manner.
Once when we were coming off the beach, our precious
Lieutenant Commander, still directing the operation,
caught sight of a girl he knew on the beach, and while he
was waving at her madly to attract her attention, he forgot
the engines and we backed right up on the stern anchor
cable, fouling one of the propellers. The Lieutenant Commander insisted on signaling for a diver, but our Captain
brushed him aside and had a conference with Boats and
Palmisano, our coxswain from Gloucester. These two and
others took the boat and, in some incredible manner I
could not see from the bridge, cleared the propeller. College men may have their points, but in some situations sea-
going fishermen, garage mechanics, electricians, and firemen are a damned sight more useful.

Soon after this episode we went north again, as far as
Mare Island Navy Yard, which is far north on San Francisco Bay. All I can remember about that voyage was
approaching the Golden Gate and trying to get through it.
Of course it's a superb sight, with those headlands, the city,
and that colossal and beautiful bridge, but when I was put

on the wheel, that was the end of sightseeing. There was a very strong tidal current running from that huge bay through that narrow passage into the ocean; we had no keel, and our engines were not those of a destroyer. We slowed down perceptibly, and when we went from full speed to flank, that helped for only a few minutes. I was finding it difficult to hold her steady on her course, and none of us knew when that steering gear would go out again. The Captain came down from the conning tower to the wheelhouse and, directing me, edged us as far inshore in that channel, on the south side, as we could safely go. It seemed likely that we'd have to go out to sea until the tide changed, but finally we picked up speed, passed Alcatraz, and headed north for Mare Island.

That shipyard impressed us tyros even more than the one at Norfolk had, perhaps because we saw evidence everywhere that a shell, bomb, or torpedo can make the steel plates of a ship about as protective as a thin slice of processed cheese. Workmen swarmed all over our ship and turned her into an incredibly noisy and dirty chaos in which we had to live and work as cleanly as we could. On the bridge we got new instruments, charts, and navigational and communications books and documents that we had to file and absorb as rapidly as possible. From this work we were often summoned to help the rest of the crew store food, ammunition, engine parts, deck gear, and everything else imaginable. Either there or later at San Francisco, great cranes put aboard our weather deck the parts of an LCT that could not cross the Pacific under her own power, and that made our fat old lady look more like an ignominious barge than ever. We were degaussed again, and also swung the ship while an old Chief Quartermaster compensated the magnetic compasses, to have them ready if and when the gyro should go out. This Chief gave me a lesson in this form of compensation, ignored by Emerson, but more than one lesson is necessary for that job. The steering gear was finally repaired successfully.

Most of us were given liberty almost every night from about 1600 to 0600 the next morning, and San Francisco could be reached by bus in something more than an hour. We knew that we were going to be in the Bay for two or three weeks, and those of us who were married and could manage it arranged to have our wives come to San Francisco. Once more, Peggy risked and managed everything to be with me, and her adventures might make a better story than this one. I found her in the restaurant of the St. Francis Hotel, and before speaking to her, I had just to look at her for a moment. We had to keep changing hotels every few days, from palaces to fleabags and back again. Peggy had some days of lonely sightseeing, and the damned alarm clock went off at 0430 every morning, but in that unique city we had some fine evenings. One night we were joined for dinner by four or five of my shipmates. Peggy liked them and they liked her, and later this made it pleasant for me to be able to mention them in letters to her, and her in talks with them. Once at sea when Ginny saw me writing to her, he said: "Tell Peggy I'm going to heave you overboard, you exhausted old goat, and come home and marry her."

During this time, we moved *456* down to Hunter's Point, much closer to the city. This made everything much easier, because we could clean the ship and be much closer to our women. Near us there was a submarine in drydock, with her crew bunked down in an old ferryboat. They had a washing machine that they kindly allowed us to use, and we discovered then and later that the submariners were a very superior lot. I heard later that when that submarine went back to work, she and all her men were lost.

When it became clear that in a day or so we were going
to shove off for where or what only God and Ernie King
knew, we moved *456* again, to a pier that was much less
thoroughly guarded than any we had seen. Our ODs were
now somewhat lax at night, and all this gave me an idea.
I asked Peggy whether she would like to go aboard, and
she—never as much awed by naval regulations and punishments as I was—said she'd love to. That night we went
down to the pier, and leaving Peggy for a moment behind
a crate, I made sure that I knew the gangway watch well—
he was Bosler, I think, and he was enchanted by the idea
—and that the OD or any other officer was not stirring out
of officers' country. We quietly slipped aboard, and when
Peggy saw me salute the ensign aft, she hesitated a moment, and then gave it a deep curtsy, which I found charming and moving. (I often wondered why so many boys
found the naval courtesies and rituals silly and onerous.
For me, they lifted us a bit out of the bilge.) We went first
to the galley and there electrified three or four boys. With
the Captain's permission, Woodall had just bought a very
good cocker spaniel puppy, and we all talked in excited
whispers about the puppy's feeding and care, a matter on
which Peggy could give Woody more good advice than you
will find in *The Bluejackets' Manual*. Woody had named
the pup "Happy," and so he seemed and so he made us.
Then after I had reconnoitered the wheelhouse, I took
Peggy up there for a minute. I didn't dare take her below
to crew's quarters, because somebody was apt to be
stripped and to let out a yell. So after Peggy had said
good-by and good luck to Woody, Bosler, and the others,
we stole ashore. My heart slowed down and I felt that
somehow Peggy had given our ship a blessing.

When I saw Peggy off on her train to San Diego—she
was going to live for a while with her brother and his

family—there were other mates and their wives parting at the same time and place. That was a grim parting, but we had had some lucky breaks and it was time to get on with the damned job.

We took on some naval passengers, and then on the morning of March 22 we fell into a small formation of other LSTs, and with signal flags flying and our bridge gang hopping like fleas, we moved out through the Golden Gate, passed the Farallon Islands, and headed southwest. At some relatively quiet moment, Ginny appeared from the radio shack, climbed up on the signal bridge, seized a hand of each of us enlisted men working there, and piled all the hands up together.

"What goes on, Ginny?" I asked.

"It is always good to do this at the beginning of a game," he said seriously. Evidently it meant that we intended to play hard together, as a team, for our ship and U.S. High. For a moment I felt sheepish, then ashamed of having felt so, and angry at Mr. Meddaugh for grinning at us sarcastically.

At some point that morning the Captain said to me: "Well, Smart, is your next book going to be called *Pacific Holiday?*" My first book was called *New England Holiday,* and I couldn't imagine how in thunder he had ever heard of it. Before I could answer, he said, "I'm rather afraid that *Holiday* will not be exactly the word," and turned away.

All of us topside at the time and not otherwise busy gave the last fading blue line of the United States, on the horizon, a long, long look.

10

The weather soon became warm and then very hot. This was before the order came out to wear clothing all over the body all the time to prevent flash burns, so many of us worked naked above the waist and got good sunburns, complete with chills and fever afterwards. Many of us let our beards grow. We had a few days and nights of rough seas, and a number of sudden rain squalls, but usually the sea and the sky were an intense blue, with a long, gentle swell and with a ring of puffy little white clouds around the horizon. Sometimes we saw flying fish by day and phosphorescence at night. Slowly Polaris sank toward the horizon and new stars, including the Southern Cross, rose up from the south; a phenomenon that added to our feeling of having moved, perhaps forever, out of any world we had ever known.

The signaling between SOPA (Senior Officer Present Afloat) and the other ships, by flaghoist and blinker during the daylight, went on irregularly for several hours a day. Sometimes this was necessary business, about our position at sea, or station-keeping, or slowing down temporarily at some ship's request (engine problems), and so on, but we also had long signal drills, involving all the ships. We knew that we were still far from as sharp as we'd need to be when working with destroyers and others in the combat zone. The Captain said, "You all are better now, but still slow—far behind the Old Navy."

My small but slowly increasing part in the navigational work continued to be my chief pleasure. Howard Gembler got in on it too, so that we became slightly furtive allies in trying out anything we could. Mr. Meddaugh was himself a good navigator, and except when he was in his worried and sarcastic moods, he helped and even encouraged us. On this voyage the work was of course entirely celestial, and usually Gembler and I could only take part to the extent of taking the time off the chronometer with a stop watch, going out on the wing of the lower bridge with Mr. Meddaugh or the Captain, and when the officer had got the star or sun or moon down to the horizon and said "Mark!," jotting down the name of the body and the time. Then the officer would work out his sights for himself. However, Gembler and I had remembered our lessons at Solomons, we had Dutton's book, and after the officers had finished, we sneaked out the sextants and did it all ourselves. Of course we were delighted when our fixes came close to those of the officers. Usually we erased ours from the plotting sheets, but once we forgot and left them there, and that produced from the Captain only a little gently laughing profanity. I was allowed to post a chart in crew's quarters and plot on it each noon position. Later, from *Sailing Directions*—beautifully illustrated, long before, by Japanese artists!—and from other books, I added notes on the history and people of the islands that we were going to see.

Maybe I became a little cocky, or maybe just exhausted. Anyway, about a fortnight out of San Francisco, I fell on my face. One of my jobs was that of getting the time-tick by radio, to check the chronometer, and to wind it every day at noon. One afternoon when I was briefly in my sack,

I was ordered up to the chartroom, and there I found the Captain and Mr. Meddaugh waiting for me beside the chronometer. I had allowed it to run down!

"Smart," said the Captain, "do you know how serious this is?"

"Yes, Sir, I do," I said, and that was a fact: I was close to heaving up my chow. After a moment of grim silence, I asked: "Sir, do you want my crow?"

"Not yet," he said, "not quite yet, but I warn you not to let it happen again. As soon as you can, get the time-tick and get it going again."

For several days I was literally sick over this episode. I was astonished when Mr. Meddaugh, having observed this, said to me once: "Take it easy, Smart, we have a long way to go." I thanked him and wished that he could take his own advice, because everyone else was finding him increasingly difficult. Evidently his experiences on the African coast had taken a great deal out of him, but most sailors could not accept as excuses any but physical wounds. I did not understand my own response to my error until one day when I found Gene Cote standing alone on the fantail with a mug of coffee and looking very sick.

"Charlie," he volunteered, "now I know exactly how you feel about that God-damned chronometer." Then he explained something that had gone wrong in the engine room, something that was entirely, he said, his own fault. "You see, Charlie," he said finally, "everyone makes mistakes, as I know very well, but this God-damned war has already cost me and my wife and children so much that it makes me sick to foul anything up, to do anything short of a damned good job." I don't think that anyone ever thought of Gene Cote and me as prigs; it was just that the situation seemed to call for as much craftsmanship as we could produce. For our own peace of mind, it also called for more tolerance of others than any of us had.

Except for accidents around machinery, ladders, and the like, our first casualty was Happy, the cocker spaniel. For some days he thrived, or seemed to. He was afraid of nothing except the testing of the guns and (properly) the edge of the weather deck, and he delighted us all. After a fortnight or so, however, he began to show worms. Our Docs tried some medicine that they said could not harm him, anyway; but it did no good, and the poor little devil wasted away until he had to be killed by the Docs and then buried at sea.

We were all depressed by this, and there was some senseless recrimination. We all seemed to get very angry very quickly, nearly coming to blows, and then to cool off just as quickly, reverting to zany backchat, totally profane, and horsing about like colts in a pasture. One way in which we could cool off physically was by climbing from the weather deck down a long ladder inside the bow to a confined place, about twelve feet by three, through which the sea water flowed about three feet deep, coming in from the bow doors and then escaping out a crack near their hinges.

At dawn on April 10, nineteen days and some four thousand miles from San Francisco, we sighted the island of Tutuila in American Samoa, and soon after noon were anchored in the small harbor of Pago-Pago. The scenery of course was exciting, with densely verdured mountains coming down to the sea. There was a lot of signal traffic, and some of us were sent to a meeting of signalmen aboard the flagship, so that in two trips I got only four hours ashore. A mate and I stood in line for one hour for a bottle of beer, and then took a walk. The natives were handsome in their skirts, and were properly contemptuous of the barbarian invaders buying beads—as we did not. However, when we passed native huts, we saw some of them eating Del Monte canned peaches, and others, Mormons or Catholics, were singing hymns with a nasal twang. We saw what was supposed to be the house of Sadie Thompson of *Rain,* but decided that such houses must be as common as those slept in by George Washington, and we did not have enough time to hunt down Robert Louis Stevenson's grave. The spectacular scenery, the long, slow surf on the reefs, the corrupted natives, the swarms of marines and sailors working resignedly as though in prison, the heat, and the languor all combined to afflict me with a sort of romantic melancholy.

This mood was quickly changed when I returned aboard. Some of the officers came back aboard tight, with a bicycle that they rode around the few square feet of the signal bridge, and then climbed the mast. Everyone sobered up promptly from liquor, or from the tropics, and began to eat out everyone else. Mr. Meddaugh reached new heights of sarcasm. Mr. Malloy and his deck gang had put a lot of black paint topside, on places that had to be touched by everyone, including the Captain, so that Mr. Malloy heard from that, but well. Mr. Carlson had sprained his ankle, which soon began to look like the cases of elephantiasis we had seen ashore. Huge old Boats was literally melting away in the heat; he said that on the whole, despite the scenery, he preferred the coast of Maine.

Somehow we got under way and took an even more southerly course, so that the stars kept changing, but also enough to the west so that we crossed the dateline. I was working always with Greenwich time, but had also to keep track of the ship's time and clocks, pushing them back. Every third day the evening watch, 1600 to 1800, was dogged—split in half, to make the watches rotate fairly.

Often mates would ask me what date and time of day it was in Albuquerque or Bangor. Despite all this preoccupation with time and place, I began to lose all actual sense of either. It was gradually becoming cooler, and I could easily imagine our going on and on, into ice floes, and then into Nothing. One night we saw flashes on the horizon, exactly every four minutes, on almost the same bearing, and we didn't know whether it was heat lightning, gunfire, or a signal from another world. Sometimes by day we were followed by magnificent birds with dumpy, mottled white bodies and long, thin, dark wings with a span of at least six feet; soaring indefinitely, they hedge-hopped the waves most beautifully. The Captain said that they were albatrosses, and I thought about the Ancient Mariner and my old Professor Lowes.

My friend Ralph Davis of the black gang had his skull shaved, lost his front-teeth bridge, broke into a rash, and was horrible to look at. He was quarreling with everyone, and I told him that he was making my mistake, that of taking everything too seriously. "You got something there, Charlie," he said bitterly. "We're all fucking clowns, falling apart and kicking each other in the ass. You remember how clowns always have this crate of a car that comes apart? Some day this ship is going to do that, and we'll all go down laughing our fucking heads off."

One night, however, while I was working in the chartroom, the Captain came in and I asked him about the proper flags in a New Zealand port. He told me, and then became chatty and said: "Smart, I'm very much pleased with my officers and men, and I'd stack you all up against any LST crew I've seen." Of course I repeated this to my mates as soon as I could, and it did boost everyone's morale, which was probably the Captain's intention.

On the afternoon of April 20, we sighted land again, at

a great distance, and it turned out to be a snow-covered mountain peak on the North Island of New Zealand. We passed along the coast and then entered Cook Strait and the large harbor of Wellington. On the way in, we were preceded by a porpoise that we soon learned was the famous one, "Pilot Jack," who guided every ship in. We spent four days in that harbor, mostly at anchor, and took on stores by boats, our own LCVPs. The holding ground was poor, and one night when I was on watch there was a stiff wind and I discovered from the bearings that we were dragging anchor. The OD rang up the Special Sea Detail, and the Captain appeared and moved her to what might or might not be better holding ground.

Despite other troubles and plenty of work, I got ashore twice and was able to send Peggy a cable. Wellington is not impressive, and we were tantalized by what we heard about the beauty and interest of the interior—and especially by the fact that it was overrun by deer while there was a meat shortage; we had plenty of rifles and ammunition, the New Zealanders had none, but we had no time for hunting. The inhabitants were more English than the English, and very hospitable. One night a good young gunner's mate from Dallas named John Tinkle and I were invited to dine at the home of a Mr. and Mrs. Ford. On the way out, by tram, we saw a pawnshop, a secondhand clothing shop, and a junkyard, all owned by people named Smart. We laughed, and I told Tinkle something my old friend Kaj Klitgaard (at that time master of a merchant ship) had said to me: that he sometimes wished he had been born a Jew, because the suffering might have purged him, as it had so many Jews, of all dross. Mr. Ford told me later that these Smarts had changed their name. It was chilly down there, and we had good food and beer before an open fire, with chrysanthemums in bloom beyond the windows.

When we got under way again, through Cook Strait toward Australia, it was cold enough to wear undress blues topside, instead of dungarees. We were all sobered by having some wounded marines on board, as passengers, and by the need to stand watches four-on-and-four-off, go to general quarters every dawn and dusk, and zigzag along our course.

It was on this trip, after examination, that Gembler, Silvester, and I were all promoted. Soon after, I repaid Mr. Meddaugh and the Captain by letting the chronometer run down again. This time I was properly eaten out and the job was given to Silvester. Again I went into a neurotic decline and dropped the steel lid of a flag bag (comparable to the lid of a trunk of a large car) on my head and nearly knocked myself cold. It was at this time that I began having a recurrent nightmare that stayed with me for more than a year. I'd find myself on the streets or subways or very high window-ledges of New York, fleeing alone from a spectral figure that followed me. This was the nasty, dirty old man invented by the great cartoonist Rollin Kirby, of the old New York *World,* to represent Prohibition, and always he was carrying a chronometer in its traveling case. The comical meaning of this dream, my need of a drink, was not apparent to me when I was having it.

Usually Mr. Meddaugh expected me to send for him when, at dawn or dusk, he did not happen to be on the bridge and the stars were ready for sights. One evening I could not leave the bridge and grabbed a Negro mess attendant and told him to go in the wardroom and say to Mr. Meddaugh: "Sir, Venus is visible." After several repetitions, he seemed to get it. After a few minutes I heard a tremendous shout from the wardroom, and later I heard that the mess attendant had gone into the wardroom, scratching his dick, and said, "Suh, penis is miserable."

11

Fatigue and exhaustion were general aboard *456* when we entered the harbor of Sydney on May 2, and we all looked forward to liberty and the feel of our feet on solid land once again. Despite the many fine yachts under sail, and perhaps because I had worked for nine hours straight— including the last five on the wheel under a pilot—I did not find this famous harbor comparable to those of New York or San Francisco. What interested me most was a fine old house and garden on the waterfront very near our mooring. I was told that this was Government House, in which in 1808 Captain William Bligh, RN, then Governor of New South Wales, hid himself under a bed in a futile effort to escape from the soldiers who had mutinied against his authority. Whether that actually was Government House and whether Bligh behaved in this manner are both points open to doubt.

We remained in Sydney harbor six days, moving the ship frequently, taking on stores, chipping paint and so on, but also having a good many hours ashore. The people of Sydney were most hospitable, and I went for example to a party given weekly by a charming old maid who lived alone in a big house. All her friends brought in food and girls, and our hostess even gave each of us a shot of whiskey, which was scarce. The correct young women did their gallant best to be amusing, but in talking with them we discovered that a great many of them had lost fathers, brothers, husbands, and fiancés in North Africa, Singapore, and elsewhere. We were impressed by the courage and generosity of these women, trying to entertain *us,* but any true gaiety was impossible. They surprised us by asking to see snapshots of our women, and one of them said: "All these American girls are *so* good-looking. It is too, too depressing." Tinkle and I were also entertained in the homes of a Dr. and Mrs. Fairfax and their son (a war correspondent) and daughter-in-law, all well-bred, thoughtful people, who delighted me and were in turn delighted by Tinkle's tall tales from Texas.

Many of my shipmates of course found female company much less correct, and a public park full of soldiers, sailors, a few civilians, and their women all making love with almost no attempt at privacy reminded me of paintings by Brueghel the elder, Rubens, and Jules Pascin. One of my shipmates got a surprise when he was walking down a street with a girl and she said: "Please excuse me for just a few minutes. It's Saturday night, and I have to step into this building and get screwed." I don't know why he waited for her, but he did, until she came out with her pay envelope for perfectly legitimate services as a secretary—*screw* being Australian for pay. Whether this courteous young woman was presently screwed in the other sense, deponent saith not. My general impression of Australians (doubtless a false one) was of strong, decent, repressed, and rather dull Anglo-Saxons ravaged by wars and sex.

In *456,* and I imagine in all the other ships, in the odd moments when our minds weren't absorbed in our work or numbed by fatigue, we were daydreaming about sexual experiences—past, future, or wholly imaginary. In our ship there was little or no homosexuality, even latent, of which I was aware. Most sailors had pin-up girls in their

lockers, and some had panties from their women. I don't
see any objection to fetishes as substitutes except that they
are almost never artistic, and hence to my taste cold and
dull. When I suggested to Mr. Meddaugh that if he'd allow
me to hang it in crew's quarters, I'd ask my wife to send
us a large and good reproduction of some nude by Cor-
reggio, Prud'hon, or Renoir, he took a dim view of that
idea. In my letters to my wife that she saved—thus for
good or ill making this book possible—I found recently
three erotic and detailed reminiscences of fantasies that
might be compared favorably, if I do say so, with similar
efforts by D. H. Lawrence or Henry Miller.

Our next center of operations was Brisbane, about four
hundred fifty miles up the coast and fifteen miles inland
from the sea on the Brisbane River, which is sufficiently
narrow and tricky to require pilots. The city itself was
dingy and dull, packed with soldiers and sailors milling
about, crowding into the bars when they were open, and
getting into fights. The LCT was removed from our
weather deck, which was a great relief to everyone, and
we were suddenly inspected by Rear Admiral Daniel E.
Barbey, commanding the amphibious force of the Seventh
Fleet, accompanied by an Anzac Lieutenant General. Although we went in and out of that river several times, we
spent most of that month, from May 11 to June 14, prac-
ticing beachings and having gunnery practice and other
drills a few miles up the coast, near a village called Redcliff. We were still rather badly disorganized and individ-
ually inept, so that the snarling on board became intense
and continuous. This was not helped by a whole new round
of inoculations, including tetanus, and an epidemic of
colds and cat fever. The weather was quickly variable,
with much cold rain.

Our general misery was relieved by a few liberties in

and near Redcliff. One night a gang of us did some pub-crawling and got involved with a gang of Australian sol-diers, some from their regular Army, covered with glory, and some from an outfit that was not allowed to leave Aus-tralia. This exemption seemed to us rather odd, since we had come thousands of miles to defend Australia as well as our own country. Gene Cote, a small man but a game-cock, raised this rather delicate point with one of the "home-bodies," as I think he called them, and soon it looked like a brawl, especially when the Aussies were led by a huge Lieutenant in their regular Army. I'm a Casper Milquetoast at heart, so I said to the Lieutenant: "Look here, Sir, this is a lot of God-damned nonsense, and you know it." That giant stared down at me, then burst into laughter, and within a few minutes everyone was shaking hands. The Lieutenant passed around a bottle of whiskey of his own, and then we all climbed into his truck and went off to eat together in some dump.

Our party broke up, and after a while I found myself lying on the grass, looking at the moon above the sea, pet-ting a big yellow dog who wanted to lick my face, and dreaming about my girl and our dogs at home. I fell asleep there, and when I awakened, still half-asleep, and started to walk toward the pier, I stepped off a cliff and fell into some soft sand and brush. My dog-friend was alarmed and came tumbling down after me, but except for some scratches, I was unhurt.

Boats came along and persuaded me to walk two miles with him to a Red Cross dance. I had only one dance, called the Gypsy Hop, with a very pretty but cold girl who sold me two tickets on a fruit cake. I'm not much on danc-ing, so I left and walked the two miles back to the pier with Doc Holt, who had been a forest ranger, and on the way we talked about horses (his true love), dogs, forests,

women, love, and war. (Meanwhile, I learned later, Gene
Cote had taken a bicycle ride and others had borrowed a
rowboat and tried to go fishing.) I had not been sound
asleep in my blessed sack aboard ship for more than an
hour when Boats and Judkins, a big, genial electrician
from Minnesota, waked me to show me the fruit cake that
I had won and Judkins had brought all the way back to the
ship untouched. When my name had been called, the Captain had sent all of our boys looking for me, while he
talked the Mayor of the town into turning it over to Boats
and Judkins for me, despite my absence. When other mates
appeared, most of the cake disappeared, but it was agreed
that we had to save one piece for the Captain.

While this was going, Freddy Medeiros sent for me
from the signal bridge: somebody aboard an LCI was asking for me personally! When I got on the light and asked
for it, the message came across: "How are you, you old
fart? Schrader." I hadn't seen or heard of him since Solomons, so that was a thrill. We agreed to try to arrange
visits by boat the next night, and this we managed somehow to do. He looked well, his bald pate was as brown as
a walnut, and he was much more relaxed, as I was, than
we had been on Chesapeake Bay. Life aboard the smaller
LCI was much simpler than aboard *456,* and in many ways
I envied him, but he was still only a Seaman First. They
had got their LCI in Houston and had stopped at many
more islands on the long voyage out. I had saved him the
last piece of my fruit cake, and when we parted, we agreed
that we were apt to meet elsewhere, up north. We had
been correcting the charts of the coasts of New Guinea and
neighboring islands, so we knew pretty well where we were
going to work.

When we went back into Brisbane, our tank deck was
filled, by others, with a sobering load of bombs and drums

of high-octane gasoline for aircraft. We told each other that if we were hit with that load aboard, we'd never know what happened. We also took aboard an outfit of Seabees, many of whom were older men from the construction trades, and although they knew little about ships and the Navy compared to us old salts, as soon as we saw them working cargo or anything of that kind, we all respected them greatly. They were much better than most of the Army units we saw doing the same kinds of dirty and skillful work.

On the way downriver again, I was at the helm, under a zany civilian pilot, who kept talking all the time, whistling, and turning his back on the river, in which a submarine, of which we had many there at the time, might appear on the surface, coming around a bend, at any moment. This pilot kept talking about politics and Rosicrucianism and quoting from *The Rubáiyát of Omar Khayyám.* Our Captain was there in the wheelhouse with us, and at first he was genial and chatty with the pilot, but as the pilot's chatter continued, he became very nervous. A Captain may relieve a pilot at any time, and must do so when he considers his ship in danger, but that is rarely done, and of course our Captain did not know that river. Finally the pilot began to quote Shakespeare at length, and when the sun suddenly appeared, he crowed:

" 'Now is the winter of our discontent . . .' " then paused, forgetful.

Those two lines had been favorites of my father's, of a sunny winter morning, so before I thought about what I was doing, I heard myself crying aloud:

" 'Made glorious summer by this sun of York'!"

"Ha-*ha!*" crowed the pilot, turning his back on the river, to face me. "Now just *where,* son, did you learn that?"

"Never *mind,* Smart!" barked the Captain. "We can do without any literary chitchat from *anyone,* in this river!"

The pilot stared at the Captain and gave a low whistle, but after that, he almost silently minded his business.

"Come left just a little bit, son," he murmured, and added sarcastically: "We don't want to *hit* anything, do we? No, we surely don't."

Naturally and justly, the Captain was very sharp with me for some time after this episode. Among other things, he beat a useful lesson into my head—in that context never to say "I think." "Hell, Smart," he cried, "you have to *know*—or at any rate, to speak up and take your chances on yourself." Or as Emerson put it in a phrase that I certainly did not quote to the Captain: "Trust thyself: every heart vibrates to that iron string." I learned that lesson on the farm, and on the bridges of ships; I may yet learn it in my study.

When we moved down the Brisbane River for the last time, we turned north and went about nine hundred miles up the coast, inside the reefs, to Townsville on Cleveland Bay. The whole coast was desolate, and once again we got an impression of that vast continent, larger than the United States, mostly barren and almost untouched by mankind. In more ways than one, we seemed to be on the edge of Nothing. Townsville is only about twenty degrees south of the Equator, so we were back in the tropics. Many of us came down again with cat fever, and most of us already had a plague that stayed with us for months: fungi on our feet, sometimes moving up our legs. There was plenty of work there in Townsville, especially in signals, since the bay was crowded with amphibious craft and also with fighting ships that we were glad to have in our neighborhood. We also had more beaching and firing, and once we saw some shore batteries doing some rather impressive firing on targets at sea. Our own planes kept diving at us, and again we wondered, doubtfully, how fast and how accurately we could get our own guns going against diving Japs.

Townsville was a hot, sleepy, dull town of shacks under a mountain. When I got liberty, I went alone. An almost empty bookstore was full of men looking for almost anything, but I managed to find three books—by Peter Drucker, Shaw, and Quiller-Couch. With these and a sandwich, I walked up the mountain and had a fine afternoon of reading and then of sleeping under a bush. Coming down, I found a bar, for officers only, and wondered, as I had before and did later, why this rather irritating special privilege was one of those considered necessary. Fraternizing could have been prevented by the "equal but separate" concept, so nauseating elsewhere. Then I much enjoyed a movie of Marquand's *H. M. Pulham, Esq.,* but the hundreds of Aussie soldiers present clearly did not begin to understand or enjoy this study of New York vs. New England character and society. On my way back to the ship, which was beached at the time, I fraternized with a fox terrier and had a hard time dissuading him from coming aboard and enlisting.

One night in the chartroom the Captain warned me about secrecy and then told me that we were going to put our passengers, bombs, and gasoline ashore on Woodlark Island, a few miles northeast of Milne Bay, on the southeastern tip of New Guinea. They were going to build an airstrip there, and it was not known whether the island was occupied by Japs or not. Then we were going to work out of Milne Bay, putting Aussies, Americans, and their gear and stores ashore, against certain opposition, at various points on the east coast of New Guinea. Nobody could face this prospect without a tremor, but after more than a year in the Navy, I found it also a relief to know that at least I was going to be on its cutting edge. I was also still very curious about "action" and my own response to it.

Some or most of our Seabees left us, we took on a capacity load of American soldiers, mostly engineers, and on June 26, with five other LSTs and maybe a couple of destroyers, we got under way.

12

The four-day run across the Coral Sea was rough, and most of our crowded passengers were seasick all over the ship. Our reliable Freddy Medeiros had somehow got a badly infected leg, so that Gembler, Silver, and I were kept hopping on the signal bridge most of each day and night. The signalmen on the destroyers were faster than we, but we managed to keep up. After picking our way through beautiful islands and dreadful reefs, our formation of LSTs managed to beach on the right island at 2100 on the night of June 30. Our soldiers went to work rapidly and well, unloading our dreadful cargo through the bow doors. We had seen only one enemy plane, very high, and we soon discovered that the Japs had departed from that island some time before. Our gunners were disappointed, but the rest of us were not. We saw only a few emaciated and staring little natives in G-strings, with huge mops of fuzzy hair and mouths stained magenta by betel nuts. We got away singly that night, and by that time the reefs had been marked by men in boats with red and green flares. The only catch was that they had put the red flares where the green ones were supposed to be and vice versa! As soon as we discovered this with certainty, we did better, of course, but there were a couple of hours in there, with ships coming off beaches, swinging around, and trying to find the channels without ramming each other, that were

worse than some hours we were to know later under actual
bombing. Finally, somehow, we got out of there into open
water under the stars.

That morning, when we were more safely under way
and the Captain was in his sack, another Captain had a
personal message semaphored to ours: "Did you ever
spend a rougher night?" Our OD at the time, Mr.
Kechijian, decided to hold that one until some real business necessitated waking the Captain. When the real business came up, I had to take it down to him, and then I
gave him the personal message also. He asked me to
semaphore back. "No. Too wild for an old man." He
looked old then, for the first time, and that alarmed me.
During the day I got four hours of sleep, a shave, a shower,
and clean, hot food. Thinking of our passengers left to
work on that island, I rejoiced in the relative luxury of the
Navy.

Sometime that afternoon, Ginny picked up from San
Francisco a public broadcast about the successful occupation of Woodlark and Kiriwina islands, beginning with a
phrase that was to become familiar: "General MacArthur's
forces have advanced . . ." and so on, without mentioning
our Admiral Barbey and the Navy.

"Don't you get it, Charlie?" snarled Ginny. "This Mac-
Arthur is Jesus Christ and, leading the way himself, he has
taught the Army how to walk on water."

That night we heard Tokyo Rose address the men we
had landed, telling them to work hard and build a good
airstrip, because within two weeks the Japs would take
over and "relieve" them. As far as we knew, the Japs still
had plenty of air power at Rabaul, and our passengers had
no antiaircraft guns. These broadcasts by Tokyo Rose
never weakened anyone that I ever heard of—quite the
contrary—but they did deepen our bitter feelings about

the General's publicity. Admiral Morison has since recorded that although this operation was a "pushover," it
was the first one of the kind in the Southwest Pacific
and "became the template for all later shore-to-shore leaps
along the New Guinea coast," by "Uncle Dan the Amphibious Man."

During the next two months, until the attack on Lae, we
saw little or no more of the enemy than we had seen that
night, but in hauling men, vehicles, stores, and ammunition
out of Milne Bay to half a dozen islands a day or two
distant, we were worked stiff and I suppose got good training. On that first run to Milne Bay from Woodlark Island
we had the job that was to become very familiar, that of
cleaning up the ship after its occupation by the heroic but
filthy Army.

Milne Bay, which we all pronounced *Milny,* is huge,
and on most of its sides the mountains, densely covered by
jungle growth, rise precipitously from the edge of the water
to the clouds that cover their summits most of the time. It
was extremely hot and muggy, with occasional sunlight
but with heavy rain for at least a few minutes almost every
half hour. From sweat and rain we were soaking wet almost all the time, and we had a constant struggle with dirty
and mouldy clothing and with the jungle rot on our feet.

The way in which the mountains descend steeply way
below the water level leaves almost no good holding
ground, a fact of which we were not wholly aware when
we first went into the bay the evening after the Woodlark
affair. I knew how to heave the lead, and Mr. Meddaugh,
who had the conn, sent me forward to take soundings. I
was heaving away, time after time, and finding no bottom,
although we seemed perilously close to the rocky shore
and the jungle. Over the phones and then with a mega-
phone, Mr. Meddaugh and then the Captain kept angrily

demanding soundings while I kept reporting "No bottom at fifteen," then twenty, and finally "No bottom at thirty fathoms!"—the length of the leadline. The officers obviously didn't believe me, and I hardly believed myself, while I became as angry at them as they were at me. I doubted whether Mr Meddaugh had ever taken soundings himself, and with a ten-pound lead on a line thirty fathoms long, no sailor ever got a sounding every half minute, no matter how bitter the cursing from the bridge. Finally Boats appeared with another thirty-fathom line that we secured to mine, and then I had to allow that giant to heave the lead himself. There was no bottom at *sixty* fathoms, and we had only a hundred twenty fathoms of anchor chain. We moved on until we finally got a reasonable bottom and let go. This time I let go myself, more savagely than I can remember doing at any other time, but Mr. Carlson and Boats (bless them) calmed me down before I got myself into trouble. That night in the chartroom the Captain remarked to me that never in all his experience had he found water that deep that close to shore.

On another occasion we could find holding ground only behind a little peninsula that concealed us from the Flag and him from us. Since signaling was almost continuous, it looked as though we'd have to station a boat off the peninsula, with flags and a hand blinker, to relay messages from and to the Flag. This would have been tedious for coxswains and signalmen, so Howard Gembler and I had another idea. We talked the OD into cooking up some kind of reasonable request or question for the Flag, and we flashed this by our searchlight on a low-hanging rain cloud. It took some time to get an answer, but finally it came, and we carried on the signal traffic in this manner until we had to move again.

In between runs, we sometimes had chances to shoot

the breeze with the soldiers, mostly engineers, living and working in the mud under the palm trees, and we didn't envy them. Their work didn't seem to be as exacting and continuous as ours, they got much more sleep, and they weren't as tense as we were, but we were cleaner, more comfortable, and better fed. Their patrols were still having a few skirmishes with Japs, but bombings had stopped. Some of the soldiers had natives working for them, and one morning I saw scores of these all lined up in their G-strings while the flag was raised: this seemed to me an absurd extension of our nationalism. However, I didn't see how these people could govern and defend themselves, in our age, any better than our cocker spaniels could, and in the last twenty years I have seen no real solution of this problem, in New Guinea or in at least half of the world.

For one of our trips, the Group Commander came aboard, took command, yelled, shrieked, cursed, abused everyone, and even ate out the Captain and Mr. Meddaugh in public. He made all of us so nervous and angry that we did our work much less well than usual. At one point he got a canvas chair and sat on the signal bridge, watching us working at flaghoist and blinker for about an hour, while saying again and again "Lousy, simply lousy." When we finally got him off in a boat, back in Milne Bay, there wasn't a man on' board who wasn't thinking and feeling deeply "Fuck you, Commander." At a formal inspection later he said we were the best LST in the Group. Months later, when I was on the other side of the earth, I heard from a mate in *456* that this Commander had made some queer mistake in piloting her that tossed our Ginny overboard and knocked him cold, whereupon this Commander dove overboard and pulled Ginny out. It also must have been this Commander who had no small part in getting me a commission. The reader may remember, in Charlie

Chaplin's *City Lights,* the violent and inexplicable changes of mood of the little tramp's patron.

Another interesting visitor on one of our trips was a war artist named David Fredenthal, whose work later became well known. On the bridge I rigged him an easel, and he painted our weather deck, crowded with men and gear. He also made some quick sketches of men at work that enchanted me, but when I tried to buy one, he told me that they were government property and could not be sold. One of our boys had some oil paints with him, and for months had been painfully copying the dreadful picture of Jesus that one still sees everywhere. I introduced the sailor to Fredenthal, hoping that this professional artist would give him some better ideas about art, but Fredenthal wasn't interested.

Life in our ship's company went on with the same bitterness and tensions. We acquired a regular Navy Chief Machinist's Mate who was less than helpful to Mr. Martin and Gene Cote. Our gunnery officer, at his request, was sent home for administrative duty, and he was replaced by a Mr. Robinson, an able and charming officer who had been a couple of years at West Point, of all places, and who confessed to me that he was appalled by our morale. What really worried me was the evident exhaustion of our Captain, while Mr. Meddaugh, next in line for command, seemed tied up in knots of inner tension.

On July 14, the blow fell. The captain had seen a doctor aboard our mother ship, the *Rigel,* and as a result was ordered home. We sent him his gear, including the commission pennant, and we never saw him again. This distressed me, because I felt I personally owed him a great deal, and like all the ship's company, I should have liked to give him a final salute. We all felt that he and Boats had been the only real seamen aboard. Mr. Meddaugh was made Captain, Mr. Kechijian Executive Officer, and Mr. Carlson navigator.

The grind of work went on, in that heat and rain, but we had a few little distractions. I saw Bob Schrader's LCI somewhere, and although he wasn't aboard at the time, I felt confident that I'd see him later. Sometimes our soldier passengers had little dogs with them, and to all of us they were an astonishing relief, although once a cute little mongrel bitch pissed on my sack. At one time we were all hammering on the edges of Australian shillings until they became rings from which one only had to drill out the centers. I made one for Peggy, but of course in my ineptitude I had to have some help in the machine shop with the drilling and polishing. Sometimes at anchor we were allowed to open the bow doors, lower the ramp, and swim off it.

To my astonishment, Mr. Meddaugh recommended me and Potter for commissions and wrote a very laudatory letter about me. Out at that place at that time, this idea seemed to me like pie-in-the-sky, of no great importance or interest. We had left San Francisco only four or five months before, but already the past and the future seemed unreal, and any other kind of life remote and hard to imagine.

The island I remember most vividly and happily is Goodenough, which I privately renamed Phaeacia. I got ashore one afternoon about 1300 and took a long walk alone. On a path through the tall grass I encountered a long line of natives: very small, with pot bellies, spindly legs, skin scaly from ringworm, and mouths all red from betel nuts. They had a peculiar rolling gait, with their toes pointed out, and they looked like a swarm of monkeys with baskets on their heads. They said "Hello" and the kids saluted. Some soldiers, passing, discussed the shapes

of the women's breasts and their extent of pregnancy with
cool detachment. Not one was a Nausicaa. I had been told
that they called intercourse *pom-pom*, would favor anyone
with it, and considered it nasty, while very few of the sex-
ravenous soldiers and sailors took advantage of the situation. When I ran into a Catholic chaplain moving his
quarters, I bore him a hand and so got a ride on a truck
farther inland. Finally I found a pool in a creek that was
clear, cool, deep enough for diving, and surrounded by
huge boulders and flowering trees. A few soldiers were
there, and they loaned me soap and a brush, so I stripped,
washed my clothes, and then had a delicious bath and
swim. One of those soldiers wore steel-rimmed spectacles
and looked like an intellectual from New England, very
far from home. He was sitting naked on a rock, wiggling
his toes, staring at them, and singing a wordless tune to
himself. I did not interrupt his reveries. It was a walk of
about four miles back to the ship, and when I came near
the beach I was attracted by a mass of hibiscus flowers
and picked a large bunch of them for crew's quarters.
While I was doing this, I was suddenly attacked by a
swarm of very large, black, vicious ants, so that I had to
bound out of the bushes, strip, and fight them off. When
I was back aboard, my mates were delighted by the
flowers, although they faded very quickly. From the stern,
on that clear, quiet evening, we saw schools of gorgeously
colored fish in the clear green water, but when the lads
were running for the fishing gear in our rafts, some great
sharks appeared and drove the fish away. With permission,
we broke out rifles and pistols, but the sharks swam away
unharmed. That night I had a watch from 0000 to 0400,
then got an hour's sleep, then saw the dawn. The clouds
had left the tops of the mountains on the island, and the
rosy sunlight touched the peaks first, then moved slowly

down to bathe the whole enchanted island and the beaches in light as we moved off and started back to Milne Bay.

Much as I enjoyed the beauty of those islands in that emerald sea and dreamed of exploring them in peacetime in an auxiliary schooner, I also found them sinister in their rankness, isolation, wild life that we could imagine, and diseased, hardly human people. I agreed wholly with Aldous Huxley that in the tropics, Wordsworth would never have found "something far more deeply interfused" that had any interest, benevolent or otherwise, in humanity. I didn't see how any sane man, even Spinoza, could "love nature" in the Southwest Pacific.

Gradually we began to wonder just what, for all our work, we had to do with this war that looked as though it might last forever. We were reminded constantly that "the enemy is so many minutes away by air," but we hardly believed it. There began a lot of scuttlebutt about a big attack coming up, but of course none of us knew anything. Gene Cote and Boats Shelton were made Chiefs, which rejoiced us all, because those two were obviously holding the ship together. I was made a Quartermaster First, but my boys were not promoted, and I felt they deserved it as much as I did. We were all made nervous by the new Captain's tenseness and exhaustion, but were reassured by Mr. Kechijian's competence and calm good humor as Exec. He would make a face at me, grin, and ask: "How's it going, Charlie?" and *then* I could answer honestly: "O.K., thank you, Sir."

Toward the end of August, we took aboard a more than full passenger complement of Australian soldiers, and many of them had to sleep on the decks. They were in their 9th Division, the remnants of the famous "rats of Tobruk," and we were proud to have them aboard. They were shy, polite, cool, and tough. The signal traffic in the fleet in

Milne Bay increased greatly, night and day. With all these soldiers on board, our fresh-water problem, always difficult, became serious. The deck gang rigged a canvas on the fantail to catch rain and let it run through a tube into a tank, but this was not nearly enough. Somehow we got our clothes and bedding washed, or got enough new clothes from the *Rigel,* to stand the formal inspection that turned out to be so successful.

On August 28, Mr. Meddaugh was ordered to the *Rigel* on sick leave, to be replaced by another Captain. To me, our parting was odd and moving. He said that he knew that all the men hated his guts, whereupon I reminded him of the fine inspection they had made for him and suggested that we all knew that every man had his limits of physical and mental strength. I also thanked him, of course, for all he had taught me about navigation, and for recommending me for a commission. I wished him luck, and as he went over the side I felt that when he had had a rest and somehow got rid of whatever vulture was eating his liver, he would make a happy and effective captain.

So that made two shattered captains, and our new one was a Lieutenant (jg) named Prue, who had been sixteen years in the Navy as a Boatswain's Mate and who looked like a lightweight boxer. With him came two other new officers, one of them, Mr. Reap, to replace Mr. Kechijian as Exec, but Mr. Kechijian took this replacement with his usual good cheer. As I had anticipated, the new Captain tightened up everything, but when Sunday came, he cut the work to a minimum and told someone that he didn't believe in any unnecessary work on Sundays. This struck me as one of the oddest and funniest things I had ever heard in the Navy, but it sounded good. It also seemed good when, on August 29, both Gene Cote and Harvey Potter had birthdays and Woody made them a birthday cake, Mr. Robinson told us it was his birthday too and joined us in a celebration in crew's quarters.

It was time for a small bit of cheer, because the rats of Tobruk were sharpening their bayonets, there were more destroyers on hand, more P–38s were roaring around overhead, and a medical officer, Doctor McLaren, had been assigned to *456*. One night Mr. Carlson and Mr. Kechijian showed me the plans for the attack on Lae, in which we were going to take part. Actually, I think we all felt a kind of relief from a very long strain.

13

Lae was about three hundred miles up the coast from Milne
Bay, and I think we may have got under way in formation,
with other LSTs and a guard of destroyers, on the evening
of September 4, 1943. Sometime that night the siren went
off for general quarters, and we all knew somehow that this
was no drill. I had hardly got my earphones, mouthpiece,
and big helmet on there in the conn beside the Captain
when the destroyers ahead of us began firing, some planes
came roaring over very low in the darkness with a peculiar
engine sound that we had been told came from Jap Zeros
only, and there were several high spouts of water off our
starboard side that could only have been made by bombs.
The destroyers didn't hit anything, we didn't get off a shot,
and I don't think the other LSTs did either. However, the
Japs had hit nothing. The black gang had asked me to keep
them posted when I could, so with the Captain's permission
I told the engine room that we had been bombed without
success. "Hell, Charlie," was the answer, "we take it all
back. You just keep any news to yourself."

I think we spent the rest of that night, part of the next
very hot, misty day, and all of the second night at general
quarters. I think we may have been bombed again that
second night, again without hits by either side. During the
next three weeks, as I remember it, we made about six
runs up that coast, to Lae or Buna, and were bombed at

least once on each lap. Our ship was not hit once, but four
of the sixteen LSTs were hit, with casualties, and put out
of action for some weeks. Several of these hits were on
crew's quarters, and after that, the crews were split into
thirds and separated among the passengers. Our gunners
soon got to work more quickly, with more warning, and
although they never scored a hit in that period, their fire
may still have saved us. Our first Captain had wisely told
us that any man who said he was not afraid under fire was
either a clod or a liar, but that every man could and would
accept his fear and get on with his job. This was proved
true. We were all very alert and very busy, if only to save
our own skins, and if our stomachs and knees began to do
odd tricks, that was almost funny, as it was when fear returned suddenly hours or days after we were out of danger.
We were bothered more by the need of sleep and the fear
of going to sleep on the job.

At dawn on September 6 we drew nearer to the coast
just east of Lae, and by this time the destroyers had all
gone ahead and were running back and forth, close inshore, firing inland, while our P–38s were swarming like
savage hawks above them and the beaches. For some reason we had to go in slowly, and by the time we hit the
beach with other LSTs in our formation, it was clear that
other landing craft had already delivered their soldiers and
cargos. Some soldiers were firing in the jungle, others were
working with their gear on the beach, and others lay dead
in a long, neat row on the sand, their faces covered. I have
never got over the sight of that, or of the bodies of young
men in the surf, and men who had seen much more and
much worse of this than I did have told me that it was the
same with them. Our passengers unloaded themselves,
their weapons, and their trucks very rapidly through our
bow doors and disappeared into the jungle.

About fifty yards on our port side there was an LCI beached, burning merrily, and apparently abandoned. It shook me to notice that this was apparently Bob Schrader's LCI. Our Captain ordered out the fire and rescue party in the boat on the port side, with maybe a dozen men under Mr. Kechijian, with all their fire-fighting gear. We saw them board the LCI and go to work with their hoses. The smoke diminished and disappeared, but by this time the LCI had taken so much water from the hoses that she was listing badly to starboard and our Captain ordered our boat to return to the ship, while we signaled a report on the LCI to the command in one of the destroyers.

A few days later in Milne Bay I was vastly relieved to run across Schrader unharmed. I think his crew had been ordered ashore and had later been taken off by a tug that tried unsuccessfully to salvage the LCI. Schrader told me that they had gone in under Jap fire, and that while the Aussies were going down the two ramps outboard on the LCIs, one of them had had his foot almost shot off. This soldier looked calmly at his foot, which was now attached to his leg by nothing but a piece of skin, while the blood spurted out. Then he remarked: 'Well! I guess I shan't need that any more," tore off his foot, and threw it overboard. Then he started to hop down the ramp, to follow his comrades ashore. Some sailors seized him, dragged him back on the deck, and applied a tourniquet, but when this had been done, the wounded man insisted on going ashore and finding his own doctor in his own outfit. The sailors let him go, and the soldiers helped him ashore.

On a later trip, I learned that that morning, or soon after, the Aussies captured a Jap hospital, and when the doctor—quite unarmed, carrying only his medical kit— went in, the Japs pulled guns from beneath their bed-clothes and shot him dead. This doctor was much loved, and the Aussies swarmed in and killed every Jap in the place.

Some of the LSTs were having trouble getting off the beach after unloading, so the destroyers came dangerously close inshore, at high speed, to create a wash that was successful. Of course we were glad then, as always later, to get off the beaches, where we should be sitting ducks, lightly armed, in case some Zeros got through our P–38s.

When we got back to Milne Bay, our morale in *456* seemed better than it had been for some time. We liked and trusted our new officers, and we felt somehow that we could go through that and maybe worse without fouling up our job. We got mail from home, promptly as usual, and of course for some among that many men, the news was bad. This time it was my turn. Peggy had had bad asthma, then pneumonia, and was in a naval hospital in San Diego. The mist that had settled around her and my past cleared just enough to allow me to see her very clearly, gasping and in danger of death, among strangers possibly callous. Mr. Carlson was very sympathetic, as was Dr. McLaren, assuring me (correctly) about the San Diego naval hospital. We promptly went back to work up and down that coast, and my memories of those three weeks are merely flashes in a long, dark struggle to keep awake and working. I am not at all confident of the accuracy of any of my memories of this period.

One evening we went in on the beach at Buna and saw there a row of fresh temporary graves in the sand, of men who had been killed a few nights before. Then we pulled off the beach and for some reason kept circling in the total darkness. We had been working so long that we couldn't remember when we had slept last, and Silvester and I were in the wheelhouse. One of us would stand up and steer, desperately, while the other was allowed to sit on the deck and sleep a little against a bulkhead. When I was on the deck I was wakened by a shout from the OD and leaped up to find Silver standing rigidly at the wheel, his eyes open but sound asleep! I grabbed the wheel and swung it as ordered, while Silver fell to the deck, then leaped to his feet and slammed his head—luckily still in his helmet—against a bulkhead. While this was going on, Zeros were buzz-buzzing somewhere, and our own guns and others were banging away, again with no score on either side. However, after we left the harbor, another LST was hit, and we were ordered to turn back for rescue work, but were then replaced on that job by a tug or another ship.

On one blazing-hot morning, Howard Gembler, Freddy Medeiros, and I were on the signal bridge, and none of us had been asleep for maybe two nights and a day or longer. I was reading off the flags of the command in a destroyer to Freddy, with his pad and pencil, while Howard worked the flag bag. Then there came by blinker a rebuke for our slowness, and the Captain was standing behind me, listening to me read off the message. He snarled something, then turned toward Howard, and by God, Howard was standing there in that blaze of light with his eyes open, hearing nothing, saying nothing, seeing nothing, just standing there, swaying slightly. "Christ!" said the Captain. "He's sound asleep! Someone take him below, and you boys just forget that crack from the can."

Then there was that Aussie Brigadier. We were going up the coast to a new landing, and our ship was jam-packed with Aussie soldiers and an unusual number of their officers. It was clear enough that the Brigadier was throwing his weight around, although in our ship our Captain of course outranked him. The signal traffic was very heavy, and this Brigadier kept complaining that his mes-

sages to his officers in other ships were being neglected
Finally our Captain handed me a message from this Brigadier to *our* flag, complaining bitterly about our neglect of
his communications. When I read this, I looked at our
Captain in surprise and anger, and he looked at me with
a wicked grin and said "Yes, Smart, yes; just send that
along as it is." So I did, and about an hour later we received an order from our flag to discontinue handling
Australian army signal traffic entirely except during one
specified hour a day, and then only if we had no communications of our own. That was the last we heard from
that Brigadier until late that night.

There were few LSTs in that job, perhaps only four,
with say only two destroyers, and as we went up beyond
Lae at night, it seemed to me that the Captain and the
other officers were not entirely sure where we were. We
had only to follow the leader in the total darkness, but no
Captain is ever relieved of his final responsibility. Finally
we swung in toward the beach, and there it was, sooner
than we thought. Another LST had beached dead ahead
of us, and her lights were flashing madly at us to *STOP!*
The Captain swung the ship sharply to port and let go the
stern anchor, and there we were on the beach, with a jolt.
Somehow the boys got the bow doors open and the ramp
down and the Aussies began to unload. I was the Captain's
talker that time, and I could tell by the way he kept
chuckling, as though to himself, and snapping his fingers
that he was nervous. He kept asking for more and faster
reports from the tank deck, and several times he went
down there himself, obviously trying to hurry the job. We
were always in a hurry, but this was different, and I remembered that the destroyers, waiting for us out there in
the dark somewhere, had not indulged themselves and us
in any preliminary bombardment of the beach and the

jungle. We heard some small arms firing. All our own guns were manned and pointed inland, but of course couldn't fire without direction. It was fairly obvious that we had beached somewhere where we should not have been, but the Captain's talker does not ask questions.

"Another report from the tank deck!"

"Everything is on the beach but two tons of bread and one Brigadier."

"Tell them to get that bread ashore and the hell with the Brigadier!"

"Tell them," I repeated, "to get the bread ashore and the hell with the Brigadier."

"Christ, Smart," said the Captain, laughing, "you know better than that!"

So we got off that beach at last, and as soon as things had calmed down a bit, I asked the Captain where we had been. He chuckled for a while, then said: "We were at least five miles inside the Jap lines, and by God, Smart, when we got those bow doors open, I didn't know *who* was coming in—the Japs or Eleanor Roosevelt!"

That was the last I heard of that little affair until years later, in a village in Mexico, when I met a retired Rear Admiral who had been a Commander in our amphibious force in New Guinea, and who still bitterly held himself responsible for our going in that night on the wrong beach. When I objected that the Aussies might have got away with it reasonably well, and that not one sailor was touched, he said:

"Not quite, not quite. A Jap mortar opened up and killed a man in that ship on your starboard side."

This still puzzles me, because I was on the conn, wide awake every minute that night, and I don't remember any such thing. Besides, it was most unlikely that I should meet that troubled veteran years later in Mexico. I don't know how so many people feel so confident that they know what has happened, is happening, or will happen at any place or time.

The grueling work in a fairy-tale world went on and on. At some time during those blurred weeks I heard from Peggy that she was out of the hospital and on her way home to Oak Hill. . . . One night I saw the whole arc of a rainbow made with pale and spectral colors by the moon. . . . Our good Doc Holt had to be taken ashore, to a field hospital somewhere up the coast, because he had some kind of a stoppage in his guts. Almost under fire, they gave him a long succession of enemas, and after he came back aboard he had to keep giving them to himself, while he suspected that this stoppage had become gangrenous. . . . One night Mr. Carlson and Mr. Kechijian asked me about Paris, and every word I said was true, but it sounded like the most fantastic lies. . . . What with corpses and rainbows, gangrene and magic islands, or maybe just fatigue and the frying heat, I found it hard to imagine anything, including my wife and home, as being real and solid.

What counted were the ship and her navigation and the unending signals; all to be kept going somehow, against battering waves of exhaustion. *Why?* At that time and in that place, even winning the war seemed remote and unclear as a compelling objective. What was clear was the behavior or craftsmanship of men like our Gene Cote and Boats Shelton, my boys on the bridge, and so many others, including the officers. This was something more and better than patriotism. This was absolutely good in itself. This was . . . art, and I wanted a little share in it myself, at least as much as I wanted someday to write a really fine little book or two. And that kind of wanting will see you through a good deal.

Then one afternoon in Milne Bay the Captain came

back from the flagship in the boat, obviously boiling, and soon after that Mr. Carlson, then Mr. Reap, then the Captain himself all told me that four of us with first-class ratings had been ordered transferred within a week to the Amphibious Force of the Atlantic Fleet! "I'm glad for all of you," the Captain said, "Who wouldn't be? But for the ship and the job we're doing, and for myself, God damn it, this transfer of four key men is a crock of shit for the birds. Now get the hell off this bridge and get Potter going on the paperwork for all of you."

The four of us: Grinnell, Boatswain's Mate First; Santarcangelo, Shipfitter First; Dubrulle, Electrician's Mate First; and I were all in a daze. The scuttlebutt was that we'd get twenty or even thirty days' leave in the States. Our mates were envious, of course, but truly happy for us and also for themselves, because this was the first break, the first real indication that all of us were not going to spend the rest of our lives off the coast of New Guinea. The next three days we spent cleaning up the ship as always, moving her here and there in the bay, and loading up—American soldiers and their gear this time—for another trip. We four lucky bastards wondered whether we'd be started on our long way home before the next job, or stay in the ship on that job and maybe get killed. We had heard too many stories about what had happened to men just before they were going home.

But on September 27, Peggy's birthday, we were ordered to pack up our gear, shave, bathe, put on dress blues, and take the boat to the *Rigel*. There were hard handshakes all around, and then there we were, standing in the boat and sweating in the rain, while all our mates crowded the rail of the ship, yelling cheerful and obscene farewells. For nearly eight months I had lived and worked in that ship, and for ten months I had lived and worked with those men, under some pressure. I knew that even if they lived and I lived, I should probably never see any of them again. I even knew that if I did by some freak see some of them again in civilian life, we'd have little in common except our memories of those months, and that such memories alone do not make continued friendship. The feelings between those men and myself could not even be called friendship in the normal sense. This was something different, narrower but deeper. Whatever it was, on that day in Milne Bay it gripped and twisted my heart.

14

I was now back in the limbo of sailors without ships of
their own, and except for a lifegiving fortnight at home,
the next four months were for me so depressing that I shall
hurry through them here. In doing so, I may tend to give a
false impression to the young, because most of a war is of
course unutterably depressing to most of the people involved in it. However, enough readers, including the more
imaginative young people, may be aware of this fact.

From the *Rigel,* the four of us from *456* and rated men
from other ships were sent to an LST that had been con-
verted into a hospital, and in this ship we spent several
days and nights mostly sleeping, until an officer caught up
with us and set us to work washing down bulkheads. We
did this with experienced slowness, while cruelly imitating
the speech and gestures of the homosexuals who seemed to
be numerous in that ship's company. We were then moved
to a destroyer being sent back to Brisbane for the replacement of a propeller that had been broken on a seemingly
nonexistent reef or on a Jap submarine that she may have
sunk. This can was so packed with passengers that we had
to sleep on the weather deck under the gun tubs; but after
our LST, that can with only one screw seemed to fly. Most
of her crew had not seen a white woman for more than a
year, and when, on the way up the Brisbane River, we saw
some girls walking along the bank, so many men rushed

to that side to stare at them in silence that the ship took on a list. In a camp at Brisbane, to my delight I found Bob Schrader also on the way home. That camp was full of sailors who had been pulled from the drink after their ship had been sunk, and these restless and rebellious men were lectured by an officer who stupidly used the classic phrase "There's a war going on."

About two hundred of us then boarded the old and dirty Army transport *President Grant,* bound for San Francisco. We slept in the huge and almost empty hold and were given only two meals a day. I drew a brig watch, 0000 to 0400 and 1200 to 1600, and spent part of that time talking with the dozen or so wretched prisoners going home to federal prisons. The most interesting of them had been convicted of raping an Australian girl whose mother, he said, was after blackmail. In officers' country topside there were a number of Australian war brides being sent home to Mom and Pop in the States. The talk belowdecks was that these girls were shacking up liberally with the officers, but this gossip could have had its source in little or nothing more than malicious envy. I found some books aboard, but was taken away from them daily for several hours by Schrader, a good new pal named Bill Smirl (a Motor Mac) and a surprisingly elegant Sergeant of Marines. These three insisted that they could teach me how to play bridge and like it, but they failed, and I haven't picked up a card since. My daily life and work seem to me to offer about all the games and gambles I can take. After twenty-two endless days and nights we finally saw that wonderful blue line on the horizon. I had been gone only seven months and twelve days, but I felt I had aged rather more than that.

Treasure Island, in San Francisco Bay, was the best shore base I had seen anywhere, but there I found myself on a very depressing work detail; packing and labeling the gear of dead sailors that was being shipped home to their families. An officer came along, said that was no job for a Quartermaster First, and took me off it. Then more shots, including tetanus, laid me low, and I developed a horrible stiff neck.

But *toujours gai!* One night Schrader, Smirl, and I painted the town red—or, say, light pink. We picked up three attractive girls and bought them a good dinner somewhere. My mates disappeared with their girls to go dancing, which my girl and I didn't want to do. Over a few quiet drinks, this girl and I had some rather pleasant egghead talk, and she seemed to me at least as normal, lonely, and sex-starved as I was. Well! . . . Then suddenly out of nowhere appeared another girl, handsome and beautifully dressed; my girl's girl-friend, obviously a lesbian and simply furious with my girl for even having a drink with a sailor! There was almost a scene between these women, but then my girl shook my hand sadly and went off with her boss. Over one more drink alone, I almost had a laughing jag over poor old Charlot's rescue from Adultery, then went back to my narrow sack on Treasure Island, wondering again when the hell I'd get orders and leave.

Having been carefully warned at Milne Bay and Brisbane to keep our mouths shut about any action we had seen, I did that until I bought a copy of *Life* with an illustrated article about the attack on Lae, including a photograph of *456* and the burning LCI.

After three days in San Francisco I finally got orders to go to Norfolk, without leave. That same day those orders were cancelled for me and others and I got twenty days' leave before reporting at Solomon's. Battered by my telegrams, Peggy shared these violent ups and downs. I waited for hours at an airbase until I got a place on a plane going to Chicago and was then bumped off it by a pretty Wave Ensign whose sweet little liver I could have eaten fried, with onions. Finally I had to take a train, and that trip seemed to last forever.

Peggy looked thin but wonderful, and *she* was no lesbian. For two weeks I was out of Limbo and in all the Heaven I ever want, but those hours ran like quicksilver, and they were strangely shadowed by my feeling of being once more a Lazarus of sorts, who could never feel quite at home again. They were shadowed more darkly by the knowledge that Peggy and I still had a long way to go through the weird, grim, endless tunnel of war.

I landed at Solomon's with a very hard thud. It was the same muddy hole, with all the old routines. In classes for quartermasters I picked up a few new wrinkles, but most of it I had learned long before. A Chief wanted me to stay there and help him teach, but when in utter weariness I agreed to let him appeal to the officers, he came back with the answer that only F.D.R. or Winston Churchill could get me off a new crew. I had lost my old crew forever, and now I was beginning the same old round all over again, with new officers and mates of whom, for the most part, I took a very dim view. When I got letters from Gene Cote and Ralph Davis, I learned that they and *456* were still slugging their way up the coast, and I almost wished I were still with them. To have them and Boats and a score of others there with me in the new crew at Solomon's I'd have given much, maybe my soul. I wrote to them, and Peggy sent them cigars. More shots and more colds, while the chill of Chesapeake Bay returned to the marrow of my bones. The only thing that cheered me was finding a boy who had been ashore on Pitcairn Island and who had with him a piece of wood from the *Bounty*—but he had never read a word of that whole wonderful and tragic story.

The depressing sense of going through the same damned routines at the same damned place was lightened by the fact that Fate repeated the good things also. Once more we were put aboard a training ship in the Bay as contemptible trainees, but this time the three stripes on my right arm and the combat star on my Southeast Pacific ribbon on my dress blues made things a bit easier for me at least. Then once more we were in Baltimore for Christmas, and with fantastic difficulties Peggy met me there again. This time we were entertained by her old friend Dr. Arthur O. Lovejoy, the distinguished philosopher and historian of ideas at Johns Hopkins, and talk with this exquisite gentleman lifted me briefly, soaring, out of the mental vacuum and fuck-you's of crew's quarters. When our crew was back at Solomon's I also got a liberty in Washington with Peggy and our old friends Bill and Helen Crosby. Washington was one place stiff with military etiquette, but again Bill, whom the reader will remember at Chicago, managed to entertain an enlisted man most royally. A few days later Peggy appeared at Solomon's, where we repaired first to the USO library. In a corner there, Peggy drew from her knitting bag a bottle of good Scotch. By arrangement, half a dozen of my new mates, and Santarcangelo from *456,* soon quietly joined us there and furtively and ecstatically disposed of most of the bottle. It was little gestures like this, in half a dozen ports, that made Peg quietly famous and much beloved among my mates on three ships.

Presently our ship's company was sent to Ambridge, Pennsylvania, near Pittsburgh, where our new ship was being completed by the American Bridge Company. Except for some shore patrol duties, we had most nights off, and I could spend them with Peggy in a hotel in Pittsburgh. Wandering around in the darkness that extended through most of the days, we heard Yehudi Menuhin play the violin and saw paintings at the Carnegie International exhibit. We also tried to dance at a USO place, but were put off the floor because somehow we were detected as a married couple! Only the correct girls brought in for the purpose were allowed to dance.

The shipyard and its workers and their mess were much like those in Vancouver, except that the workers on our ship chipped in and bought us a washing machine that was inadequate but a godsend. Also, our new ship had many more 20-mm. guns and a number of twin-mounted 40-mm. guns, complete with a fire-control system, replacing the old five-inch gun on the fantail that had not proved effective. Besides, as I learned later with vast relief, this steering gear was not defective. Whatever this ship's company might be, the ship itself might be much less vulnerable than those working out of Milne Bay.

On January 22, 1944, United States Ship *LST 138* was put in partial commission and we all said good-by to our women, but we knew we had a good chance of seeing them again before we went overseas, probably to Europe. The next day, with a Coast Guard warrant officer as pilot and with a smaller secondary crew on board to teach us the ropes in the rivers, we started down the Ohio.

15

That trip down the Ohio and Mississippi rivers was fun of a poignant kind for all of us. I say poignant because many of us had come from farms and old country homes and city slums like those we saw on the banks of the Ohio; people kept waving to us, and it could well have been our last good-by to all that. Except for the deck gang, getting us through the numerous locks and onto the Ohio, the work was relatively easy. A special temporary rig had been installed in the conn so that the pilot could steer the ship and use the engine-room telegraph from there. His knowledge of the rivers was uncanny, and we took soundings only before letting go the anchor, which we did every night. With its numerous curves, its wooded hills coming down to the water, and its rich history—as at Marietta, Blennerhassett's Island, and elsewhere—the Ohio River seems to me one of the noblest that I have seen. At first the Mississippi was disappointing; just a big, muddy river full of shoals, with mud- or sandbanks, scrubby trees, and only a few huts visible, but soon enough, somehow, it became weirdly impressive, perhaps because of the very emptiness of the scene. By some magic, this LST in 1944 had moved back a couple of centuries into the wilderness. Then suddenly there was the city of Memphis, with all the tall buildings lighting up in the dusk.

My big moment on that trip came one evening when I was taking soundings for the pilot. Some thirty years before, when I was a small boy visiting my aunt at Oak Hill, I read *Life on the Mississippi,* in an illustrated copy of the first edition, every summer. It seemed to me quite wonderful that I, an aging literary gent, was now taking soundings in the great river. As the water slowly grew more shallow, I waited eagerly for the surface to touch the two pieces of leather on the lead line that indicate two fathoms. For this the Navy cry is "By the mark two!" but I cried with all my strength "By the mark *twain!*"—and I hoped that shout of homage and gratitude was heard in Heaven. The pilot jumped off his stool in the conn, and I could see him laughing with surprise and delight. "Let *go!*" he cried, and down went the bow and stern anchors. In my experience, river pilots and those in the Panama Canal, who have inherited the mantle of awe and power worn by the Mississippi River pilots in Mark Twain's youth, are more individual and humane than naval officers as a group.

We arrived at New Orleans February 2 or 3, and there the holiday of sorts ended. We kept moving the ship in difficult places, and Mr. Kleinhans, my new Communications Officer, kept coming aboard with navigational gear to be stowed and tons of communications data to be filed and charts to be corrected. There was also of course the tonnage of stores to be taken aboard and stowed by all hands. When some welders came aboard, we had to remove all the ammunition to the dock, then replace it in the lockers after they had finished their dangerous work. We learned much later that several LSTs had been blown up by welders in that fateful place, Pearl Harbor. While I was lifting ammunition, I felt a pain in my groin, and a few days or weeks later, I discovered that I had ruptured myself. For the rest of the war this was only a very tiring nuisance except at one point, when it came close to interfering with me most seriously.

It was while I was on one of these jobs that I should perhaps have taken advantage of the kindness of a huge and gentle gunner's mate named Iggy Czubas, who had been a professional boxer before the war and who said to me, "Charlie, I know you don't like to think you're old, but this job is too much for you. You can just hit your sack, because I can do the work of two, and nobody will know the difference."

In this crew I had been alarmed and depressed by the number of men who seemed to me to have been overrated on shore bases and by the number of boys who seemed to be guttersnipes from the North, or trash from the South. Besides the familiar tension and bitterness caused by lack of confidence, the crew's quarters had a tone—say of fuck-this-ship as well as fuck-you—that I didn't like. The good will and sense of responsibility didn't seem to come down from the officers and rated men and dominate the mental climate as it had in *456,* and from what I could see of it, the wardroom didn't seem to be any better off. However, by this time I had found some good men and good mates, and began to hope that my impression was false or the climate would change. Besides Iggy Czubas, there were Charlie English, a shipfitter and plumber from St. Louis who was as good at his job as he was at gold-bricking when he felt like that and who had a wonderful sense of humor; Rusty Reisig, who had worked on the Great Lakes and whose brother had been killed in the Pacific; Doc Markle; and a number of others, including my green but hard-working boys on the bridge, Churgin, Kehl, and Hanshaw. My immediate boss, Mr. Kleinhans, was also green and young, but a sensitive and sympathetic type, like other of the young officers. The only real sailor among them was Mr.

Tucker, the Engineering Officer, an old Navy Motor Mac who had gone into the drink with the *Wasp*. The Exec and navigator, Mr. Bollenback, had also come through the hawse-hole, but evidently only from a desk in ONI. The Captain, Lieutenant J. B. Wilson, also seemed to be inexperienced, but he was a big man of incredible stamina, doggedly determined to learn. Once again, we men and our officers could only hope and try for the best.

On one night only, Charlie English, Doc Markle, and I got over to the city. We liked the old houses and bars, we drank imitation absinthe, and we listened to some jazz that even I, no enthusiast, found very good. On February 4 we were put in full commission, with a ceremony and even a band on the tank deck. I was pleased when the Chaplain did not ask God for victory or safety, but for "clear eyes, steady hands, and high hearts." Remembering New Guinea, I thought we'd need all three, as well as more knowledge and seamanship than—except by Mr. Tucker —I had seen displayed by anyone in our ship's company, including myself.

After only a few days in New Orleans, we went down the river with our own crew only, but with a pilot. When we came out into the Gulf and the pilot's boat took him off, Mr. Bollenback told me to lay out the course for Galveston. Although vaguely anticipated and feared, this was something of a shock. It was not Mr. Bollenback's fault that he had not been taught his job, and I was lucky that I had learned a good deal of it. Although inshore navigation is more dangerous than offshore and the Gulf has tricky currents, I thought I could do the job, but I found myself at once, and for months afterwards, in a position that was difficult and embarrassing both for me and for the officers. The Captain's confidence in me, and his patience with me, were great, and I appreciated them fully, but he did not trust his officers to conn the ship (he did that job himself almost all the time, with a dangerous minimum of sleep), and he kept me there beside him on the conn, or on the bridge, or in the chartroom, at all times except when there was obviously little danger—and then I had to get some food and sleep, and also get on with the signal job, the endless paperwork, and my part in all the drills. Besides, I had often, when they were allowed to do anything, to explain things to the young ODs, and even to warn them not to forget this or that. On the whole, they took this odd situation very well indeed, but it must have been as awkward for them as it was for me. I have to admit also that I had my moments of bitterness over doing an officer's work without an officer's pay, authority, and few privileges, especially when in this ship I somehow had little of the comradeship that I had enjoyed in the crew's quarters of *456*. Once more I was saved only by the interest and thrill of the job itself, by intense concentration on charts, lights, the weather, and beautiful instruments and calculations.

At Galveston, civilian workmen swarmed over the ship night and day, filling her with filth and hideous noise, while Churgin and I worked desperately on the charts, *Notices to Mariners,* and the familiar flood of documents from Washington. Degaussing again, and we got our first radar, which we hoped would be as good as it was supposed to be. The weather was foul, and except for beer and seafood during the few hours we could go ashore or wanted to, Galveston seemed to us a dump. Finally we got the ship cleaned up and got under way for Panama City, on the northwest Gulf coast of Florida, about three hundred miles east of the delta of the Mississippi—where I was depressed by seeing mud from my own farm in Ohio ten miles from shore.

At Panama City we had ten days of "shakedown cruise," which is necessarily one of the toughest jobs in the Navy.

We were all working up to twenty hours a day, on every kind of drill and maneuver I had ever heard of, and a few more, usually with higher officers from shore on board to instruct, watch, and criticize, which they did with zest. The weather was balmy, and the harbor and beaches would have been lovely for painting if there had been time and tools and if the shoals, mists, and sudden rain-squalls had not often sent me, as a navigator, into cold sweats. By this time the Captain was very tired and irritable, and once or twice, after I had offered facts and opinions for which he had asked me eagerly during many days and nights, he said that when he wanted my opinion he would ask for it. All tempers were getting short; Captain's Mast was busy; and Charlie English had to improvise a brig.

During that shakedown we pulled two memorable goofs; the first one, in its way, was funny. When the Captain made his first beaching alone, which is comparable to a first solo flight, I was his talker, and the boy on the phone on the stern had an extreme Southern drawl. The Captain let the stern anchor go far too soon, so inevitably, like doom, the final drawl came up to the conn: "Nine . . . hundred . . . feet . . . of . . . cable . . . out. . . . There goes the . . . *anchor!*" It weighed a ton and a half and was by no means a throwaway item of merchandise. While the ship was on the beach, and after she came off, I was sent out in a boat, with some boatswain's mates, a grappling hook and line, and another line with a weight and a wooden float, to locate and mark the stern anchor, which would have to be recovered later by a tug and some real seamen. We finally caught the cable and then worked back and forth along it until we found the anchor and marked its location with the float. When I reported this, as ordered, by semaphore, some wag on the bridge signaled back: "Bring the anchor aboard." We were not amused.

By our next goof, nobody was amused. We were moving
the ship in the harbor at night, in a mist, and I or somebody else must have had some doubt or made some error
about the lights and bearings, so the Captain sent me forward to take soundings. As I was doing this and reporting
them back to the conn through talkers on the phones, the
water grew steadily more shallow, and I began to shake
with anxiety. Then the order came down: "Belay soundings!"—stop taking them. This seemed to me the last thing
imaginable to do; I'd have kept the soundings coming
while slowly backing out of that place. However, my opinion had not been asked. The next thing was an unmistak-
able slight tremor of the whole ship, and she stopped moving: we had indeed run aground.

The Captain tried to fishtail her off astern, and then
even drove her forward, with no success at all. We reported
by blinker or radio, and that night and throughout the
three days during which we remained there ignominiously,
officers from ashore swarmed all over us. Everyone worked
like a demon within his realm and capacities, and the Captain, no jerk, quietly let it be known that he blamed nobody but himself. Ballast was pumped, all our fresh water
was dumped, and I think we even unloaded all the ammunition into a barge. Nothing worked, and finally a great
deal of the oil that we had taken aboard in Galveston had
to be pumped out into a lighter and (I heard) sold cheaply
to some salvage character. Then a Navy tug pulled us off.
Meanwhile, a regular hearing by a Board of Inquiry was
held in the wardroom, and my turn came to appear there
alone before six or eight officers, in dress blues, to tell my
version of it and answer questions. After that, one of the
inquiring officers took me out in a boat and ordered me to
take and report soundings, obviously in order to find out
whether I knew how to do so. He made no comment, and

I heard nothing more about my part in this affair. All hands were pleased when the Captain was not relieved of his command, and ever since I have half regretted that I did not simply ignore his order to belay soundings.

Somehow we staggered through a few more days of that shakedown, then went back to New Orleans. Part of that run was by night, and we were made anxious and angry by the lights from burning gas from wells along the shore, because these lights made it very hard to pick out the lighted navigational aids. I had managed to telegraph to Peggy from Panama City, but only by bribing a Chief temporarily on board from the shore base with a quart of alcohol from the supply in my charge for floating the cards in the magnetic compasses. He named his price, and I knew I could get more in New Orleans. There we worked ourselves stiff again, with stores and documents from shore, in the midst of the usual dirt and racket made by civilian workers adding what we hoped vainly were the final touches to the ship.

Finally one night I found Peggy in a hotel lobby, where she had been waiting for many hours with a bad cold. There was no room for us there, but after following up many leads, including one to a place that turned out to be a whorehouse, we did find a room. After that bad beginning, we had a few very good hours together, whenever I could get ashore. Sometimes we explored the French quarter in the good company of Charlie English and his Winnie, down from St. Louis. Charlie genially called Peggy and Winnie "our two old bags," and it amused me to see my New England lady, as well as her husband, being educated in other kinds of manners and language, often as good as ours or better. When our women left us, I knew there was a fair chance of my seeing Peggy again in New York or Boston, before we went overseas.

16

At that time, I was not yet sure whether I was actually going to be the navigator of that ship. Mr. Bollenback, or one of the ensigns, might know more than had been apparent. We left New Orleans on March 15, and soon after we had dropped the pilot at the delta and taken my course for Key West light, I found out. We were alone, and proceeding by dead reckoning alone seemed both unnecessary and foolish. After waiting a while for some officer to get busy, I suggested to Mr. Bollenback that I was a bit nervous about the accuracy of the chart showing the currents there in the Gulf, and that he might care to begin getting some sun lines. (My God, I thought, if the squadron commander, wherever he was, could hear *this* conversation!) He agreed, hesitantly, so I handed him a sextant, took the time off the chronometer (which I was *not* forgetting to wind!), and led him out on a wing of the bridge. He fumbled around a bit and finally said "Mark!" after which we went back into the chartroom to work it out. Once there, he said wryly: "Smart, you'll just have to carry on." The vagaries of Bupers in giving jobs in a hurry to millions of landlubbers were obviously much rougher on many officers and men than they ever were on me. In fact, except when one of us let the other down, I sometimes rather fearfully felt myself accompanied by Pallas Athena.

With Churgin holding the watch for me, I shot the sun

every hour or two for a while, advancing one line against another, and got fixes that seemed reasonably good and that indicated that if we stayed on our compass heading at that time, we'd sight land or smash into a reef a good many miles north of Key West. We couldn't do that until the next afternoon, but still, I didn't feel like keeping this curious bit of information to myself until I could get a more reliable fix from several stars, should they be visible, at dusk. I could imagine Mr. Meddaugh looking over my shoulder at the plotting sheet and laughing at me sarcastically, and I wished he were there. Apparently there wasn't an officer or an enlisted man on board who could check my work. I went up to the conn, and without mentioning Mr. Bollenback, I explained the situation to the Captain, who immediately ordered the change of course I had recommended. He also ordered me to have a cot put in the chartroom, to arrange the signal watches without myself, and to remain on the bridge or in the chartroom, unless briefly relieved by himself alone, whenever the ship was under way. That evening I got a good fix from the stars that confirmed my doubts about the current chart and that necessitated another small change of course. The next afternoon I figured we'd sight first a buoy, number so-and-so, off Key West, in say an hour and forty minutes, on such-and-such a bearing. This I reported to the Captain, and then I got his permission to go below briefly. I took a leak, had a cup of coffee, and stretched out on my own sack. I was far from sure about that damned buoy. Celestial navigation still seemed to me close to the miraculous, and I had seen and done enough of it in the Pacific to be aware of the dangerous residue of uncertainty.

Finally I went back to the bridge and joined the Captain and the OD with binoculars. Nobody said anything until a buoy appeared, at just the right time and in just the right place. Then the Captain took the ship closer to it, to be sure of its number, which was correct. I had the new course ready in my mind and on my lips. Silently, I thanked the friend of Odysseus.

So far, so good, but thinking of the months and dangers ahead, I wanted someone to learn enough to check my work and be able to replace me. With the permission of my immediate superior, Mr. Kleinhans, I found the Captain in the cabin, in one of the rare times when he was there, and asked him to assign one of the officers to me as a navigator's striker. (Again I thought wryly of the squadron commander.) The Captain agreed and asked me which officer I wanted. I chose Mr. Kleinhans, but the Captain said rightly that he would be too busy as Communications Officer, and gave me instead Mr. Bruml, an Ensign I had not previously much noticed. However, the Captain told me that until he informed me of a change, I, and not Mr. Bruml, under himself of course, would be responsible for all matters of navigation. Mr. Bruml was a tall and intelligent young man from Cleveland, a graduate of Antioch College, and he worked out very well in this abnormal and difficult situation, in which for a long time I had to teach him on the job and sometimes, in a pinch, to say simply "No, sir" and brush him aside. Many but not all the young officers in such situations, of which I hope there were not too many, must have shown Mr. Bruml's good sense and good taste.

On that voyage around Florida and up the East Coast to New York, Mr. Bruml, Churgin, and I, not to mention the Captain, had an exciting arduous workout, which incidentally kept my mind off what seemed to be the poor organization and what certainly was the sour morale of the ship's company. The force of the Gulf Stream was variable and not accurately known. The east coast of Florida was at that time strewn with the wrecks of merchant ships that had been popped off like ducks by U-boats when seen against the lights of the cities, dowsed criminally too late. Twenty years before, I had been in a hurricane off that coast farther north, and without celestial sights, we had come near Cape Hatteras. We had no such bad luck in *138,* but tyro navigators and skippers in the Navy seem to sweat more than some old hands, such as the skippers of the *Andrea Doria* and the *Stockholm.* The new radar we had was a boon, but those things are hard to read with confidence, especially by raw hands, and then and later (when I had more control over them) I thought the young officers trusted radar too much, as compared with their own eyes and brains. When we picked up Ambrose Channel Light and then an experienced pilot, the relief of all hands was extreme.

We spent nine days in or near New York, mostly at a North River pier just west of Greenwich Village, and then at Bayonne, New Jersey. Peggy arrived with her parents and managed to find rooms in a hotel in the Village, while I got a good many nights of liberty from the ship, which was once more made a mess by civilian workmen. Those were very strange and emotional if happy days and nights. Years before, I had lived and worked there as a literary hack, and now I was walking those streets in a sailor suit.

One afternoon on the corner of Eighth Street and Sixth Avenue, I ran into e. e. cummings, whom I had never met, but to whom Peggy and I had once sent a crate of fresh eggs in gratitude for his poems. I introduced myself, and this excellent poet and man was most cordial to me. "Oh, *yes!* the superlative egg-man from Ohio, but why, oh *why,* this odd costume?" He invited me to his place for a drink, but to my eternal regret, shyness made me plead another date that did not exist.

Then one night before Peggy arrived, I took Charlie
English to the Harvard Club for a drink before I dined
with my mother on Long Island. From the club, some good
radio broadcaster took Charlie to a big fight at the Garden,
and very late that night, Charlie burst into crew's quarters
superlatively high and happy with the news that at the
Stage Door Canteen he had been dancing with Katherine
Cornell. "You dumb bastards never seen such quality as
that dame! 'Tell me, Charlie,' she said to me, 'tell me about
the plumbing business in St. Louis.' 'Kit, darling,' I said
to her, 'when I'm dancing with you, I'm no plumber, I'm
a sanitary engineer, with wings!' " Flying shoes finally shut
him up.

Then one day I took Peggy and her parents to lunch at
the Harvard Club dining room that is open to women.
There I was suddenly kissed by an Englishwoman, very
chic, whom I had known years before in Paris, and who
had been a close friend of the American girl in the fashion
business, with whom, to my immense good fortune, I had
been living at the time. This Englishwoman drew me aside
from my startled family and from her suspicious escort, a
banking or legal type, and told me that the girl of my
youth in Paris, who I knew had lost a lung from tubercu-
losis and escaped from Paris through Spain to her home
in Montana, had died there the day before. There was
nothing more to be said until Peggy and I were alone together on a bus going up to the Metropolitan Museum, and
then the woman of my whole life said it only by gripping
my hand. If I could imagine and weave together strands
of life as implausibly yet movingly as Fate does, I could
write one good novel before I die.

Soon after, Peggy and I had our last coffee together at
dawn, in a little joint on the waterfront that we had visited
on less grim mornings. This parting wasn't any easier than

the one in San Francisco, because it was clear enough to everyone in March 1944 that our side was going to take a crack at the Nazis in France. All we could tell each other, as so many millions of others were doing, was that every day and night brought us that much closer to the end of the war.

I didn't go ashore from Bayonne, where we cleaned up after the workmen and made ready to get under way. On the afternoon of April 1 we cast off with a pilot and several hundred soldiers on board, crossed the harbor under the towering buildings, and started up the East River for Boston. The pilot was a genial and competent little man named Mr. Zabeline who gave Mr. Bruml and me some excellent shoptalk. Also on the bridge there was a Navy doctor who kept asking me about the different buildings, and especially about Doctors Hospital, where my nephew and niece had been born only a few years before. This pleasant doctor was killed, on another ship, on D-Day. It was even stranger for me when we went up Long Island Sound and I could see clearly the Creek Club, where my sister and her husband had often taken us swimming, wining, and dining. At dawn we went through the Cape Cod Canal, where some early risers stopped their cars and waved to us. Somewhere near the Boston lightship I took a signal from the pilot schooner, passing on to us an order to turn the pilot over to them, then join a convoy, which we knew was going to Halifax. It was very cold, gray, and misty, and this time that lightship was the last of the United States.

17

After going up a long, narrow channel with desolate, rocky scenery on both sides, we anchored across the harbor from the city of Halifax and near a grim building we were told was an insane asylum. The weather was mostly dark and always bitter cold. We kept up the usual drills in our own ship, and there were also many signal drills among the many Canadian, British, and American ships of all kinds anchored there. These were necessary because a system had been invented for combining the British and American procedures with as few changes to each as possible. One day all my lads and I were sent over to a Canadian corvette to take a lesson in the new system. We stayed in that harbor thirteen days, and Churgin and I spent much of that time correcting charts and plotting on them, from what I think were called Queen messages, the known minefields, Allied and enemy, in the English Channel, the North Sea, and other areas. This was tedious, hard work but clearly important, and Churgin and I took great care with it. We were much disgusted when, soon after we arrived in England, we received on board a whole new set of the same charts, with the minefields printed on them! Of course these also had to be kept up to date from the Queen messages.

I had only two or three liberties in Halifax, and didn't want any more, because it seemed to be a very cold, grim, and dull city. It was also almost bone-dry, except for a Canadian petty officers' canteen into which we were warmly welcomed by the Canadians. Their beer seemed warm and heavy, but it had plenty of alcohol. This fraternization was by no means universal, and elsewhere than in that good canteen, some of our mates got into terrific fights. I don't think Iggy Czubas, our ex-pro, indulged himself in this way, but our yeoman, Charlie Platt, a Golden Gloves champion, really enjoyed himself. *Ai!* That was a cold, rough town.

On April 18, to the relief of all hands, we got under way in a very large convoy of maybe sixty ships, LSTs and merchant ships, guarded by maybe half a dozen destroyers and corvettes and a baby flattop, all Canadian. By day the signaling was constant, with the Commodore always eating everyone out for bad station-keeping. Because the weather was mostly thick and rough on that passage, station-keeping was very difficult, especially at night, and I did not envy the Captain or the young officers whom he now, from sheer fatigue, had to allow to do some of the conning. Of course we got our positions thrice a day from SOPA, which exempted me from the critical decisions, but Mr. Bruml and I were kept busy in bad weather getting the positions we had to signal to SOPA. We both goofed now and again, but Mr. Bruml was coming along well, and I looked forward to his being made the real navigator, but that didn't happen until much later. We went to general quarters for a long time every dawn and dusk, and at every alarm. One of the merchant ships had to drop astern because of engine trouble, and never did rejoin the convoy. We heard later that she had been torpedoed and sunk, but that all hands except those killed by the torpedo had been picked up by one of the corvettes.

Somebody goofed in setting our course, because the au-

thorities presumably kept track of the icebergs, yet we saw
two of them. The first appeared late one afternoon and was
impressively visible above the ships clear on the other side
of the convoy. Then one morning just before dawn, when
I was on watch, several ships up forward began unaccountably and alarmingly to play around with their search-
lights, which of course was fine for any U-boats in the
neighborhood. They had good reason: the vast, gray,
looming, eerie shape of an iceberg slipped right through
that convoy, only a couple of columns away from ourselves. Once more we were grateful for the shallow draft
of our LSTs. Just after sunrise that same morning we
sighted a spouting whale, and I startled the OD by singing
out "Thar she *blows!*" She or he was a brown monster, at
least forty feet long, with a square head—"and sperm at
that!"—and she came plunging by us only some fifty feet
or less on our starboard side, so that we saw even her big
eye and the hole through which she was blowing. I have
seen whales in the Pacific, but never so close, and no old
print or book exaggerates the impression of animal power
and mystery. I saw not the evil of Moby Dick but something very much alive and very mighty that will never be
found in a zoo. We also ran into a real storm, with waves
higher than our eye level on the bridge, which was thirty-
seven feet above the waterline; great, driving hillocks of
solid water, breaking at the crest, and often with pale sunlight gleaming on them as though on hammered metal. I
am by no means an adventurous type, and I loathe camping, but I shall go to sea again when I can, if only as a
passenger, and if only at the age of ninety-nine to cheat
the doctors and the undertakers by leaping from the stern.

Presumably to evade U-boats, our convoy made a long
run toward Spain, then another long one far north, so that
our landfall was off the northwest tip of Ireland. It so hap-

pened that neither the Captain nor Mr. Bruml nor I was
on the bridge that afternoon at that moment, and I was
furious with the OD and less silently so with the quartermaster of the watch, as well as with myself, because nobody had got the precise time and bearing of that landfall.
In that convoy this error had no practical importance, but
it was lousy workmanship and seemed to me to reduce our
bridge gang and officers to the level of the galley boys, who
a few night before had got into a fight and thrown several
dozen eggs at each other and all got Mast. My God, I
thought, what a ship. It spoiled the thrill of the first sight
of Europe, which I had not seen for eleven years.

Soon we sighted the coast of Scotland and ran down
through the North Channel past the Isle of Man into the
Irish Sea, and so into the harbor of Milford Haven on the
southwest tip of Wales. That is a handsome harbor, surrounded by hills, and the gorse was in bloom. I didn't get
ashore there, but with binoculars I could watch the sheep
on the hills and examine the country houses, wondering
which one had been inhabited by Peggy's ancestor, Mrs.
Benjamin Rotch. During the Napoleonic wars, this Quaker
lady had gone to Europe with her husband, a shipping
magnate, and had been so seasick on the way that she had
never returned; at Milford Haven she had unwillingly
entertained the notorious Lady Hamilton. Whatever our
ship's company might be, that beautiful countryside,
soaked in history, would be better than New Guinea.

The convoy had been broken up, and during that month
of May we moved mostly alone, I think, from harbor to
harbor, eastward, along the south coast of England. I
could not, of course, report in my letters home where we
were, and to my surprise, I have since found the logbooks,
now in the National Archives, equally reticent. In any
case, our alertness and efficiency on the bridge were in-

creased by our moving alone in those crowded waters without running lights, and by the report, later verified, that two LSTs loaded with soldiers and on some kind of drill had been sunk by German E-boats in those very waters.

In Plymouth our tank deck was unloaded in a surprisingly leisurely fashion by longshoremen, and we got a fair amount of time ashore. Perhaps because the *Augusta* and other major ships were there at the time, there was a lot of signaling and moving the ship, and there was more formality than we had ever encountered elsewhere. Once we had to line the rails at attention in the unheard-of combination of undress blues and flat hats, and sometimes our mail was delivered to us by English Waves, very smart in their boat; they always got plenty of cheers and wolf-calls. The destruction of the city appalled me, and although the pubs had almost no liquor, the people in them and on the streets seemed to me very polite and friendly, as well as tired and brave. My admiration for the British was not at that time shared by many of my shipmates, although later it was by almost all of them. Once when one of them drawled some snide and ignorant crack about the limeys, I told him to tell that to the Luftwaffe, then wrap it in the Confederate flag and stuff it up his ass—a suggestion that might well have got Charlie Smart, despite his age, a broken jaw.

My mates' response to the English was notably altered when some of us were most hospitably taken into their homes. On two afternoons a Mr. and Mrs. Talbot served tea to four of us enlisted men and Mr. Tucker in the walled and luxuriant garden of their old house in a village near Plymouth, and that kindness and the gentle beauty of the place fed and fortified all our souls. On the second visit we took our new friends five pounds of tea, and Mrs. Talbot gave me a huge armful of flowers of many kinds to take back to the ship. When we were walking through Plymouth in the very late dusk, an old woman grinned at me and my flowers and said, "It's love what mikes the world go round!" I made a big arrangement of them, in a pitcher, for the crew's quarters, and some lad said, "By God, Charlie, I bet they ain't got nothing that good in the *Augusta!*"

All the waters around the Isle of Wight, Southampton, and Portsmouth were densely crowded with fighting, amphibious, and merchant ships of all kinds and sizes, and since many of them were manned by sailors at least as inept as ourselves, we had plenty of hair-raising moments and exhausting hours on the bridge. That display of sea power made it clear that we were going to be in an operation much bigger than I had seen in New Guinea or perhaps than anyone had ever seen anywhere. It impressed and cheered me so much that I risked encouraging Peggy by sending her a clipping of a photograph of Hitler, screaming, under which I wrote: " 'Was this the face that launched a thousand ships and burnt the topless towers of Ilium?' " Presently I was summoned by the officer-censor to the wardroom, where he asked me what the hell I thought I was doing, putting military information into a letter. I said that those were nothing but two lines from an old English play, and I suggested that they could hardly supply anyone with new and precise information. He let my letter go.

We moved down eastward, and one morning about 0330, when we were near Dover, I was awakened by the ominous sound of the engines going into reverse. I dashed topside and found the Captain doing the same. Although he had a small British patrol craft as a guide and Mr. Bruml beside him to warn him, the OD had rammed into the Dumpton buoy—British buoys are named, not num-

bered—on the notorious Goodwin Sands. I began to wonder when and how we'd sink that ship. About that time I
took the written test for Chief Quartermaster, and because
I ignored all the questions about the navigational gear in
destroyers and more complex ships, I flunked it, I was told,
by a narrow margin. I didn't give a damn about the rating
as such, but I wanted the higher pay for Peggy. The Captain and I were back at work together almost all the time,
and once when he shouted some question down the tube
to me in the chartroom, I told him I didn't know, and when
he exploded, I explained that as a Quartermaster First I
hadn't got that far in the book. "Smart," he said, "you'll be
a Chief in three days. Now do you know the answer?" . . .
"Yes, Sir, and thank you," I said, and told him what he
wanted to know. I don't like blackmail, and I liked and
respected that man, but I wanted very much to get into the
big attack and out of it and then out of that ship.

When we were anchored in the Thames Estuary off
Southend, interesting things began to happen. We beached
somewhere and took aboard a load of tanks and part of
the Elgin Tank Regiment from somewhere in western
Canada. I think this regiment was part of their 3d Division. One of the soldiers took me inside one of the tanks,
and I was glad I wasn't going to be deafened, then fried
alive inside one of those things. We were issued gas masks,
and promptly shaved off our beards so they would fit. We
were also issued hot, sticky coveralls to wear on deck as
protection against the liquid gas that might be dumped on
us from the air. There were no liberty parties after about
May 30. Charlie English remarked: "Cheerio, boys!
Cheeri-most frightfully-o! This little party is going to be
ruddy hot, right out of the fucking old Nazi pot!"

On June 2, Mr. Bruml came aboard with an unusually
large load of charts and publications that this time, he told

me wryly, he had to digest himself. With the Captain, he
took them into the cabin, and a Canadian soldier with a
rifle was posted at the door. An hour or so later I was sent
for, and the Captain told me to memorize all the material
that we might possibly need as well as I had learned anything in my life, and to say not one word nor hint about it
to anyone. Then they left me alone with the operational
plans for D-Day, June 5, with special reference to our part
in it. We were going in on one of the Juno beaches, relatively far down east, near Courseulles and within a few
miles of Caen, which I had visited thirteen years before on
a bicycle. I was relieved to see that we were not going to
be in the first wave, but was glad to see that we were going
in on the great day. Our superiors, from a Commodore all
the way up to Ike, were British, and we were now opera-
tionally a part of the Royal Navy. The size and complexity
of the whole operation, the thoroughness and detail of the
planning and the data supplied us—including, for example, photographs of our beach from close offshore and
what proved to accurate information about the sands and
tides—all this, plus the knowledge that this information
was among the most dangerous and valuable kept secret
(if it had been) in history, sent shivers down my spine.
Also, I was rather staggered by the amount of information
about minefields, channels through them, buoys, and lights
that I had to memorize with absolute certainty. From those
nights on the New Guinea coast, I knew that in a pinch
there would be no time for me to look something up on a
chart or in a book. After a few minutes of "wild surmise,"
I went to work.

Some time later I was interrupted by a Royal Navy
Chief who had some additional documents and who oddly
insisted that I, not the Captain, had to sign for them. When
I saw that the receipt was made out for "His Majesty's

United States Ship *LST 138*," I paused, only half laughing at myself. Then I refused to sign it, and told the Chief to remind his officer of the year 1776 and a sailor named John Paul Jones. When the angry Chief objected that I could merely cross out *His Majesty's* I said that I shouldn't presume to tamper with a document of the Royal Navy, and advised him not to try it himself. Disgusted, he went back in his boat to wherever he had come from, and later returned with a new receipt.

Everyone knows that the attack was postponed twenty-four hours. (On June 6, 1952, when I was on a newspaper junket to Abilene, Kansas, I was standing within a few feet of Ike when he startled me, at least, and alarmed me about his possible Presidency, by recalling his great decision and attributing our relatively good luck to the intervention of God.) On June 4 or 5, all hands not on watch were mustered on the weather deck and what was said was also piped to the Canadian soldiers below decks. The Captain made a brief statement about the operation, and then an English chaplain who had joined us read a number of prayers out of the Book of Common Prayer. He had a magnificent voice, and I was moved, but I was also irritated, because when he prayed for "our sovereign lord, the King" he did not also mention the President of the United States. When the Captain asked me what I thought of the service, I said that I thought it was good but regretted this omission. To my dismay, because of the redundance and the men standing, we went through the whole thing again, this time with the President mentioned. I had been a smarty-pants once too often. We were also handed printed and eloquent final exhortations by General Eisenhower and Admiral Sir Bertram Ramsey, RN. Rusty Reisig said, "Well, if we aren't squared away now, we never shall be." Although I suspected correctly that none of our mail would go out until later—when the Navy compassionately sent home first the letters written *after* the attack—I wrote to Peggy that this looked safer than it had been in New Guinea.

At 1340 on June 5, overcast and misty, we got underway for France.

18

Presently we found our place in a very long formation of ships that remained in one column, as I remember it, until we were past Dover and joined other formations during the night. When we turned south and dawn came, we found ourselves part of the biggest fleet I had ever seen. Although we saw only a small fraction of the thousands of ships involved, they seemed to fill the Channel in all directions. Overhead, all moving south, there were thousands of aircraft with stripes painted under their wings for identification, and they turned the misty sky into an enormous banner by their plumes.

Like others on that day, I felt great pride in being a part of this vast force that since before midnight had been striking down one of the great evils and shames of our time. Besides, I had been very happy in France, among people who seemed to me then, as they do now—despite all their failures in government—among the most civilized on earth. Their underground had fought back with incredible courage and stamina, and now the cleansing of France was at hand. And like others, I thought of Crispin's day and "We few, we happy few, we band of brothers," while being glad that we were not all *that* few.

That we were not on a stage or on a picnic was made clear enough, out there in the middle of the Channel, when we passed two bodies floating only a few yards off our starboard side. They were handsome young RAF officers in their lifebelts, with their pink faces upward, washed over by the steel-gray water. What had happened to them and their aircraft we could have no idea. I thought of their families in England who did not yet know, and who were perhaps at that moment kneeling in prayer for them in ancient churches. The Captain made a signal about them to one of our escorts, and soon we could see those bodies being picked up.

We sighted the French coast at 2130, while it was still light. The ships of all kinds were very dense, and they, the buoys that had been set out for our guidance through lanes that had been swept for mines, and the reefs along that part of the coast all kept us very busy and alert on the bridge. Evidently the schedule of landings there had been held up by the fighting there earlier that day, by the work of demolishing the mined traps on the beach, and by the tides, because we received an order to anchor in a certain position and await further orders. This we managed somehow to do, in the fading light and then darkness torn by flashes of gunfire.

It is a curious fact that during those hours and until we were on our way back to England I experienced a period of calm and complete self-confidence that I had not known before and was not to know again during the war. I knew at the time that under those rather difficult conditions, the Captain and I were not going to make one mistake in piloting, and we made none. This had nothing to do with the slight personal relation between him and me. A similar experience recorded by members of aircraft crews is included in Aldous Huxley's *The Perennial Philosophy,* but I cannot ascribe to mine any religious meaning. I can only wonder.

All hands wanted to go right in on the beach that night,

as we had expected to do, and the Canadian commanding officer paced our bridge in a suppressed rage. All of us topside felt hot and silly in our gas suits, and the Captain allowed us to take them off. That night just before midnight and then again a few hours later, our ships were attacked by a very few enemy aircraft—I think they were Ju 88s coming in low—and at least three were quickly shot down. Our own gunners banged away with delight, but really had no chance to score. The next day we saw many more corpses of British soldiers in the surf; they were being picked up by boats. A Royal Navy cruiser, perhaps HMS *Edinburgh,* appeared and anchored not far from us, on the sea side, and began firing all her guns directly over us at invisible targets on land. When she fired a broadside, that whole ship recoiled and our own ship was shaken, while the shells going over us made an odd whooshing sound. We liked to think of those shells blowing up Nazis waiting for our Canadians, but after some hours, this firing became a nuisance for those of us trying to snatch an hour or so of sleep between long periods of critical work on our feet.

Finally, sometime after midnight on the morning of June 8, we got orders to go in with our load, on the sector of the beach assigned, and we had to pick our way through a mess of Nazi obstacles and sunken small craft. When we hit the sand with bow doors opened and ramp down, there was still too much water there to permit the tanks to go. The Captain sent me down to the ramp with a lead line, and although the water was going out fast, the Canadian commander stood beside me fuming. I had made up my mind that I was going to be the first man from that ship to touch French soil, so when the mark required by orders was reached on my lead line, I told the tank officer to let them go, then I leaped in and waded ashore. The tanks came right after me, and as soon as they got on dry land they scared the daylights out of me with explosions that came from nothing but a device to clear some kind of water-repellent skin the tanks wore. The tanks pushed rapidly across the beach and disappeared in the dunes. The beach was littered with broken junk of all kinds and thick with steel and concrete traps. Before rushing back to my job, I said *"Vive la France!"* to nobody and hastily filled a pocket with sand. Some of this sand I later mailed back to the Talbots at Plymouth, England, and to my friend Dudley Fitts in Massachusetts, to make their cats' sandboxes the most chic in the Western World. As our last tank disappeared, we all waved them good luck, which they needed, because that outfit must have been in the heavy fighting in that sector before Caen fell, more than a month later.

The tides, which had been predicted accurately to the minute, did not allow us to get off the beach until 1039 that morning. Walking through troop quarters, I found a copy of George Santayana's *Egotism in German Philosophy,* left there by some unusual Canadian soldier whom I could only hope was not at that moment being killed by the egotists. During that wait, I heard later, several of our lads sneaked briefly ashore until Mr. Tucker, on watch on the ramp, saw one of them pick up a Nazi anti-personnel bomb for a souvenir! Mr. Tucker yelled at him to throw it as far as possible and drop to the sand. Luckily he obeyed at once; when the bomb hit something it exploded, but nothing touched that lad or anyone else. Soon after we had come several hundred yards off the beach, we suddenly saw floating a few yards from our bow an enormous mine, perhaps six feet in diameter, with projecting detonators, that may have been intended for large ships like the *Edinburgh,* and that could have blown us to the moon.

The Captain moved carefully away from it, seaward, while we signaled to one of our British watchdogs, which moved slowly toward the mine. How they got rid of it I don't know; there was no explosion before we got out of there, fast. That afternoon, in a convoy, we started back for an anchorage somewhere near the Isle of Wight.

Such (so far as I know) was our very modest and relatively safe part in the great attack. As Stendhal and many others have discovered, the men in a battle—and especially those on its margins, like ourselves—know little about it. I have read several accounts of what happened on and off Juno Beach, June 6–8, and they all differ a good deal. Some call it a pushover, others a shambles. What I know is that the men we saw dead in the surf had willingly risked their lives to give the rest of us the years we have had since. And just what has each of us done with those precious years?

There is a footnote that for me illuminates a little the dull clowning in *Henry V*. It may have happened back at our safe English anchorage, or even on the French coast while we were waiting to go in, and our wives, having heard the radio, were praying for us little tramps and clowns. Implausibly, we had received from above a request for qualified volunteers for bomb-disposal work. None of us was anywhere near qualified, and only one, the brave, brainless lad of the antipersonnel bomb incident, showed any interest in *that* job. English, Platt, Markle, and others, including myself—the Pistol, Nym, Bardolph, and Fluellen of our day—forged an elaborate questionnaire for this lad to fill out, including such questions as "Write here the name and address of the person to whom you wish to have sent any posthumous medals you may receive." Even after we explained the word *posthumous,* our victim filled in every blank, while we treated him with unusual respect, tinged with awe for his heroism. Before the joke went too far, we got an officer to order the lad to appear on the quarterdeck for a medical examination by Doc Markle. Doc began with his feet, then rose with a long sigh and told him that he was disqualified, because his feet were so horny that he was apt to walk on bomb triggers without feeling anything unusual. I don't think that he ever discovered the fraud. When the work is brutal, so are the necessary jokes.

19

During the month that followed D-Day there was a sharp letdown in our morale and efficiency as we were kept busy taking aboard heavy loads of men, vehicles, ammunition, and all kinds of stores, chiefly at Southampton, and delivering them on the different French beaches and mulberries. One night we saw what seemed to be a very heavy bombing of Cherbourg. One day on the French coast we saw a stockade full of German prisoners, and I confess that I'd rather have seen the lot of them lined up dead on that beach, in rows, as I had seen the Australians at Lae. Once we had to leave one of our boats, manned, on the French coast, for several days and nights of some kind of duty, and when we were finally able to pick up those boys and their boat, they were hungry, filthy, and exhausted. They told us that they had nearly been thrown into an improvised brig by some Beachmaster because they needed shaves and their white hats were dirty! Once some of us got ashore in France and hitchhiked a few miles inland. I wanted to see what the lovely Norman countryside looked like after "liberation," and of course it was very grim and depressing, with most of the farm buildings and trees at least half demolished, the fields churned up, and a few sad-faced peasants trying to take care of their animals. Our own gunners wanted to see some artillery in action, but when we found ourselves walking along a road with hedgerows but within sight and sound of firing, I told them that I for one didn't propose to let myself get killed as a silly sightseer. I turned back, looking for another Army truck returning to the beaches, and my mates came with me. Caen, heavily reinforced, was holding out week after week, while our boys, as we heard much more briefly from the British broadcasters, were slugging their bloody way to the west. Once more, as it had in the Pacific, it seemed as though the damned war would go on forever. (It was about this time that Anne Frank and her family in Holland, who had been cheered by the news of D-Day, were hauled off to their deaths in a German camp.)

Our own temporary relief came unrecognized at the time, and ignominiously. During the 0000 to 0400 watch on the morning of June 24, when we were moving south somewhere near the Needles, at the western end of the Isle of Wight, and I was working in the chartroom, our whistle sounded and a flurry of orders came down to the wheelhouse from the Captain on the conn. I rushed out to the starboard wing of the bridge just in time to see a merchant tanker bearing down on us on a collision course. The Captain swung our ship hard to starboard just in time to prevent our being rammed at right angles amidships, but we did get a blow in the starboard quarter. The ship that had hit us disappeared in the darkness astern without answering our blinker, and the only means of identification anyone saw was her British red ensign. The First Lieutenant rushed below with deckhands to investigate and handle the situation, which from what I heard did not sound serious.

When I was relieved at 0400 I went below and found that we had been hit in the sick bay. There was a jagged hole that extended from the deck, just a few feet above the waterline, to the weather deck above, and the sick bay was in chaos. Seated alone together on the deck of the sick bay, in sloshing water, tight as drums, and singing "Bollicky Bill the Sailor," I found Charlie English and Doc Markle. Doc had been asleep on the operating table when he had been awakened by a jolt and found himself staring at the bow of another ship within a foot of his head until it pulled out and away. After some efforts had been made at shoring up the hole with beams and mattresses and everyone else had departed, Charlie and Doc had discovered that the ramming had sprung open the sick-bay safe, which contained the only liquor on board. I got the bottle away from them and some coffee inside them, heaved the bottle overboard—at great pain to myself—and talked Charlie into getting some of his lads and going back to work on the shoring. When the Captain appeared, they were hard at it and I was staring at the scene as though I had just seen it for the first time.

We went on to France in that condition, and when we returned to Southampton got better repairs in a yard, but we were still hardly seaworthy. Returning from the next trip to France in a large formation, we got an order by blinker to join the part of the formation that was going to the Thames Estuary. To my astonishment, the Captain ignored this order and continued in the group headed for Southampton. "Christ, Charlie," a signalman muttered to me, "the Old Man must have something good in Southampton." Within a few minutes a British destroyer came dashing up to us on our starboard side, and her skipper addressed us sharply through a bullhorn. Ours called attention to the hole in our side and said that he intended to get repairs in Southampton. The can's skipper replied simply: "Sir, you have received my order and you will execute it." Then he went about his business while we joined the group for the Thames. We were still very clearly His Majesty's United States Ship *LST 138*.

It was night when we came into the Straits of Dover and saw our first V-1 or buzz-bombs, which had short tails of fire. The RAF boys were after them and we saw one bomb explode in the air over the Straits and another over Kent. The next day, to our relief, we did not stop in the Thames Estuary but with a pilot were sent on up the river to London. Once again we had the Captain-pilot situation, with the Captain getting very nervous while the pilot, with the aid of a tug, took us through tricky narrow channels between warehouses into the Royal Victoria Docks. Soon after the tug left us and disappeared around a corner, a buzz-bomb came over very close, its motor stopped for the dive, and my heart stopped with it. There was a heavy explosion, and we heard a little later, from a deliberately casual official on the dock, that our tug and all her men had been destroyed. We were moved several times until we were finally settled down in a small drydock, right on the river, for repairs. Soon after we got there, another bomb hit a building nearby and our boys found pieces of it on our deck; it was sheer luck that none of us was hit. I picked up one hot, jagged piece, wrapped it in a rag, and slipped it into my hip pocket until I could mail it to the Ross County Historical Society. Then I forgot it until I sat down on it, got a nasty cut on a buttock, and heaved the damned thing overboard, while Mr. Bruml, laughing, said he would get me a Purple Heart. During those weeks two other LSTs, moored side by side right across the river from us at a small American naval base, had their sterns blown off, with a number of men killed and wounded. We suspected that the Nazis knew more, and had better marksmanship with those bombs than at that time they were commonly supposed to have. One of our boys said, "Hell, Charlie, let's go back to the nice, comfortable beaches of France."

The usual swarm of civilians came aboard to repair our hole and turn the ship into a noisy mess, while Churgin and I went back to our endless chore of keeping the charts and publications up to date. It was a relief to go topside from time to time to join the gang chipping paint off, putting more on, and watching the barges and other traffic in that filthy but fascinating river. The forms and colors, in the ever-changing weather, were lovely, and I could understand why for centuries so many artists, including even the Venetian Canaletto, had been enchanted by that river. For a while I expected another Board of Inquiry into the ramming; but only a British Commodore appeared, he seemed genial, and I at least heard nothing more about that affair. Years later, I read Churchill's explanation that Boards of Inquiry into the numerous rammings of ships manned by inexperienced officers would have taken most of the experienced officers from both navies, paralyzing the fleets.

There in London for nearly a month we got plenty of sleep for a change, and also a good deal of liberty, usually at night but often enough in the afternoons as well. With British Double Summer Time, there was daylight until after 2200, but then the blackout was total. Our ship was miles east of Westminster, and we used to catch buses or rides in jeeps through the vast area of docks, warehouses, and slums that had been severely damaged by bombs and fires in 1940 and later. The area around the east end of St. Paul's was mostly rubble so that I felt that I had never really seen that great church before, and I hoped vainly that a cathedral close would replace the debris. Of course there were plenty of ruined houses all over the city and suburbs, even as far away as Kew Gardens, where I spent a few hours alone, enjoying the gardens, birds, and tired lovers who merely gripped each other more closely when we heard bombs explode somewhere nearby. I was lucky in having some old friends in London, and sometimes with mates, I did what sightseeing I could, but like them I spent a good many hours just walking or riding around and sitting in pubs and parks, watching the people, including the crowds of huddled figures sleeping in the Underground. For four years these quiet, reserved but friendly people had been getting on with their lives and work in great danger and under endless difficulties while their homes were destroyed and their friends and relations were being killed on every continent and sea, or around the corner. Near-exhaustion was clear in most faces and bodies, and several times I saw women burst into tears on the street. I felt very proud to be there with them, in uniform, without a passport or money, in their time of trouble, having done what I could in a ship. One night Charlie English did more; he worked all night among the wardens, pulling living and dead people out of a hospital that had been hit by a bomb. Those people would never give up or collapse, but in those long evenings and black nights punctured by explosions, I wondered how long, even after victory that seemed certain though slow enough, the civilizations achieved through centuries could beat down and outlast the barbarism around and within them.

The first chance I had, I looked up my old and dear friend Walter West, a printer whose home and shop were in Mitcham, on the Surrey edge of London, and whose younger children, four years before, he and I had arranged to have escape from the bombs to Oak Hill, until the Nazis sank a ship full of English children and Churchill had to stop that whole operation. Wally's good partner-brother

Horace was then in the army in Egypt, and Wally was somehow carrying on the shop with boys and old men who worked at night as wardens. Not long before, the Wests' house had been blasted, so they were living above the shop. They welcomed me with great good cheer, but while we were having high tea, the bombs kept coming closer, and Wally moved us all, including about ten printers, into a tiny shelter they had built in the back yard. Packed in there, they all made quiet jokes, but then I saw that Wally's aged mother, who had been bombed out of two houses, was lying there weeping, and somehow that old woman's plight made me more angry at the enemy than anything I had seen anywhere. Several times I was able to go back to Mitcham, where this one sailor had an English home.

One night I was walking down a narrow street near Shepherds' Market, I think, when a bomb came over low, in the dusk, and I couldn't resist looking up for it. That was the last time I ever did that trick. The engine stopped, and the next thing I knew, someone had tackled me and thrown me into a doorway, while the bomb exploded somewhere nearby and a shower of glass and rubble fell into the street. My rescuer, whose face I could not see, pulled me and himself to our feet and said, "I shouldn't try that again, mite, and excuse the tackle. I suggest you go in that pub and have a pint." "You come with me!" I said, but he thanked me and disappeared in the gloom.

The pub was almost pitch-black, with the air full of dust and people lighting candles. The place was crowded, and everyone was acting with marked nonchalance. When I finally got a pint and was standing there alone in the crowd, drinking it, I noticed in one corner a table occupied by three; a nice-looking old lady and gentleman, and with them, seated solemnly in a chair, their black-and-white spaniel. In front of each of the three there was a small pewter mug, and when the lady and gentleman lifted theirs, the spaniel took a couple of laps out of his own. Most English people were much more friendly to strangers than they had been years before, and I couldn't resist approaching this charming threesome.

"Excuse me, Sir," I said, "but my wife and I have spaniels at home in Ohio, and I'd be most grateful if you'd allow me to buy your friend a drink."

The old gentleman smiled, looked at his dog, and said: "That is most kind of you, but I suspect that on the whole Roger would feel better tomorrow morning if you allowed him to buy you a drink. Won't you please take that other chair?"

We had some good dog and country talk before parting, and Roger's mistress said: "You wouldn't think Roger was only nine years old, would you? He was born and raised in Essex; he has never liked the city, and the bombings have aged him, poor dear."

Another old friend in London was Howard Whitaker, a paper manufacturer in our home town, at that time attached to the American Embassy on some kind of economic mission dealing with the neutrals. Whit was as full of keen, informative talk and good humor as ever, he knew the few good places to eat and drink, and he allowed me to pay often enough to save my not very notable pride. Once when he fed Wally West and me, it came out that one night a week Whit was serving on antiaircraft guns in the Sixth City of London Rifles, which had been one of Wally's outfits in the first war. (Years later, we three old veterans renewed our friendship in Ohio.) Whit had an apartment on Grosvenor Square, and one night I found myself in the elevator alone with a civilian who had a fine, rugged, sad, American face; Ambassador Winant himself.

He greeted me, and I wanted to ask him whether he missed his wife and cocker spaniels as much as I missed mine, but I was too shy. We exchanged a few words and wished each other luck. Mine, alas, turned out much better than his.

One afternoon Mr. Tucker and I went to town together, and because the art galleries were mostly bare, I suggested that we go to Old Bailey. The main courtroom had been bombed out, but there was a trial going on in a white tiled room in the cellar. The royal arms had been fastened to the wall above the bench, and the judge and barristers wore gowns and wigs as usual. More importantly, justice was being pursued as usual, intelligibly and with scrupulous care and fairness. A little Jew named Cohen was accused of having made a false claim for fifty pounds, to the War Damages Commission, that his apartment had been damaged in a raid. His guilt seemed almost obvious to me, but the barristers on his side were at least as numerous and sharp as those for the prosecution. When Mr. Cohen took the stand, the ancient judge, who had a bad head cold, addressed him courteously just before he took the oath, to point out the seriousness of that oath and to assure him that if he, as a member of the Hebrew faith, wished to wear his hat while taking it, the court would take no offense. As the trial proceeded, every now and then there would be the heavy, muffled thud of the explosion, somewhere above and near us, of a bomb sent over by men who were burning Jews and who, while boasting of their culture, could not have understood this trial at all. When that thud came and the walls shook a little, the talk would stop for a moment, then calmly proceed.

Mr. Tucker and I did not see the end of it, but went out to investigate the little antique shops near the Inns of Court. He got an old gold coin and I two very small old silver liqueur cups in which Peggy and I could toast each other, if we survived. Then we went to a new Noel Coward movie, *This Happy Breed,* all about dear old England. It included a noisy sequence about the bombing of London by zeppelins in the first war, and while this was going on, we heard two actual bombs nearby, and everyone in the audience laughed aloud. When we came out, Mr. Tucker remarked, "Charlie, I suspect there was more of the real England in that trial than in this movie."

One afternoon I went on a real errand for the ship with Mr. Bruml, and after we had done it and managed to get a couple of whiskies somewhere, we decided that we wanted to see the Admiralty, so we boldly went there and asked for a chart that we already had. We were treated most courteously by some officers and a Chief who were almost as charmingly antique yet impressive as the building itself, which was hit by a bomb the next day.

Because of his humor, curiosity, sympathy, and zest, I always enjoyed roaming about with Charlie English when we could get liberty together. One night in the Underground he found a small boy amusing himself by trying to draw, while his mother slept there beside him. A few nights later, Charlie miraculously found the same boy and gave him some paper and charcoal he had bought for the purpose. One afternoon Charlie and I managed to get out to Hampton Court, and although the palace was shabby and stripped bare, in the town we encountered an eccentric old antique dealer who dragged us into his shop and bet Charlie a guinea that neither of us could identify a piece of furniture he insisted on showing us. I spotted it as Chinese Chippendale, and wondered later aloud to Charlie why the old man had risked a guinea on anything so obvious. Charlie laughed and said: "The old fucker was obviously trying to take us, so I decided to take *him.* I told him I was a plumber and you were a street-cleaner!" Back in

London, at the Charing Cross station (I think), we used some gargantuan baroque urinals made of marble and Charlie was awed and delighted. "They should put floodlights on them and charge admission," he said. "The guy that made these was the Michelangelo of the trade. I wish I could show them to Kit Cornell."

Toward the end of July, despite all our sleep and liberties, we all became increasingly restless and rough with each other. We hated the disorder, the make-work, and the setting-up drills on board; and running into American sailors who had been at Anzio and Salerno, we may have felt an *extremely* slight touch of guilt over being mere sightseers in London. However, the job on our hole was nearly done, which was more than could be said of the war.

Perhaps my oddest adventure in London was my last one. One evening I was sitting alone in Green Park when an American Army First Lieutenant stopped in front of me and asked me whether I wasn't Mr. Smart. I stood up, saluted, and said, "Yes, Sir," while trying to remember his face. "I'm Chad Gilpatric," he said, "and I was in your Fifth Form class in English at Choate, about eleven years ago." I remembered him then, but well, and we sat down and had a happy talk about those days. Then I had to go through the usual routine of explaining as well as I could why I was wearing a gob-suit. It soon appeared, however, that the Lieutenant's interest in me was not wholly personal. He had seen the quartermaster's chevrons on my arm, and he said that he and his superiors needed a good quartermaster in the worst way. Besides, hadn't I told his class about bicycling along the northern coast of France? How well did I remember that region, and how good was my French? I answered these questions honestly, but he said: "By God, I think you're just the man we want," then finally told me what for.

Gilpatric was in an outfit, mixed Army Air Forces and Navy, that was in the business of recovering airmen who had been downed in France, and who were being hidden, cared for, and delivered to the north coast by members of the French underground. Gilpatric's outfit was sending men disguised as French fishermen and harbor bums over to that coast in submarines and PT boats. These men would go ashore in the darkness, find their way to certain villages, and get in touch with the underground people, who would then turn over the airmen for prompt and quiet return to the boats and to England. It was a very successful business, Gilpatric said, but they needed men who looked older and more plausibly French, and above all, who had had some experience in strange coastal waters in the dark. Then of course there was another little angle to the job; prisoners were needed for interrogation, and when kraut sentries were encountered, the trick was to seize, disarm, and gag them, then bring them along—or else, of course, if need be, to kill them, quietly, and keep moving. I may not have remembered it all accurately, but it went something very much like this.

Well! . . . I explained to my old student that shivers were running down the spine of Mrs. Smart's little old boy, who had never been near a Jap or a Nazi, and who had never learned how to kill anyone quietly. Gilpatric laughingly brushed this off, flattered me by saying that I looked tough enough to him, and explained that they had a very good school in which I could learn the commando tricks in a few weeks, while also brushing up on my French and picking up a little German. I wondered for a moment whether all this wasn't a gag on an old schoolmaster, but Gilpatric hadn't been that kind of a boy—Jack Kennedy had been—and he seemed earnest and plausible, fantastic as this turn of events was in my life. I wanted to get out of

138, and for a moment I may have had an extremely fleeting and sardonic case of Steig's "dreams of glory." In the end I told him I'd take the job, if he really wanted me, whereupon he told me that I'd have lunch the next day with some Commander and himself; an official Navy order would be sent to my ship early the next morning. Grinning —at what?—we shook hands, saluted each other, and parted.

Scared, exhilarated, and yet not quite believing any of it, I found my way to a pub, then back to my ship in the darkness. When I got back aboard, I promptly learned that we were going to get under way the next day!—and of course nobody was going ashore again. I had a wakeful night, and the next morning I saw the Captain and told him privately about my talk with Gilpatric. He snorted and said, "Smart, your friend had better get those orders here damned fast. Frankly, I think you're going to stay right on my bridge." While my gang and I got the bridge and chartroom squared away, the morning wore on without— as far as I knew—anything coming aboard that had anything to do with me. Finally I got the OD's permission to go ashore as far as the nearest telephone booth. I called Gilpatric's office, but he wasn't in, and for security reasons the only message I dared to leave was that if Lieutenant Gilpatric wanted Smart, he'd better act fast.

As we went down the river that afternoon, I wondered whether it had all been a gag, and whether I should ever again see my friends the Wests and the heroic city of the western world.

20

The next month, August, we spent working between Weymouth and the various French beaches, and the work seemed hard, dull, and unending. The slackness on our jobs, the snarling in the crew's quarters, and the relations between the officers all seemed to grow worse, while for my part I didn't seem to be learning enough that was new to me about navigation, signaling, or anything else to keep my mind and temper serene in spite of it all. I have thought a great deal about the morale of ship's companies, and the determining elements may be these: (1) the luck of the draw; whether the key commissioned and petty officers are mostly of the kind that would be good, and set the tone, in almost any circumstances; (2) whether the ship's company has been trained together long enough and well enough to make most of the officers and men feel confident of themselves and of their mates; and (3) whether the commanding officer has enough skill, experience, self-confidence, and humane good will to make a good ship in spite of bad breaks in the two matters above. In the case of *138,* I was myself a difficult odd-ball, and I was not then and am not now in a position to criticize my officers and mates. I wondered then, as I do now, whether it was not simply a matter of someone's having shot an albatross.

Weymouth, however, was a pleasant town, very clean, with many parts of it almost pure eighteenth century, with bow windows, window-boxes full of flowers, and so on. Also, it had been relatively undamaged by bombs. My mates and I got into the habit, whenever we had enough liberty, of catching almost any bus going out of town and getting off at some village or country pub. These were usually less crowded than those in town, and in them we had some chance of getting an ounce or two of whisky before the beer.

In one such pub, while my mates were throwing darts with English sailors, I got into a conversation with a quiet little civilian whose wife's father had been the brother of Thomas Hardy and the Warden of the prison on Portland Bill, across the harbor from Weymouth, the prison in which Hardy had pictured the hanging of Tess of the D'Urbervilles. We talked at length, but since not everybody shares my passion for Thomas Hardy—acquired, I hope with my students, at Choate—I shall report only that this man said that Maugham's *Cakes and Ale* was very considerably true to Hardy's life, at least with his second wife.

Once, instead of going to France, we spent a day running up and down the coast just east of Weymouth, above instruments that had been sunk there to test the pressure produced by different kinds of ships in passing at different speeds. This was done because the Germans had developed "oyster mines" that were exploded by pressure. It seemed to me, to my delight, that I had seen just that bit of coast in a beautiful painting by John Constable, and the RN Commander directing the operation confirmed this surmise. He also told me how poorly that coast had been defended in 1940; he thought that the Germans could have invaded Britain successfully, if with much slaughter, and that if they had done so, the war would have lasted forty or fifty years. On another evening I was able happily to try out my French on an officer from a Free French destroyer that had come into Weymouth. He had escaped from Lille in 1942. In his view, Oran could have been avoided, Petain was *merde,* and the United States was a complete matriarchy.

One liberty episode of that time was painful, and I have remembered it often during the last two years. One evening Charlie English, Rusty Reisig, and I went out to a village and found a very attractive pub. We were having a pleasant time with English soldiers, sailors, and civilians when we were most unluckily joined by an acquaintance of Rusty's from another LST. His previous LST had been sunk under him in the Channel, and he was very nervous and excitable, also Southern. In came a group of American Negro soldiers, one with a handsome blonde English girl. I managed to keep our party quiet about this until the Negroes and the blonde left, and until we were ready to leave ourselves. Then I noticed that our nervous sailor had left before us.

When we were out in the country lane in front of the pub, we found him on his back in the road, with three Negroes standing over him, one with a switch-knife open in his hand. Since I was the senior petty officer in our group, the lead was now up to me. First I sent Charlie back to the pub to telephone for the MPs. Then Rusty and I walked slowly towards the weirdly motionless group there in the road. The last thing I wanted was a fight, and especially a racial one, there in that hospitable and quiet English village. If there were a fight, the pub might very well lose its license. On the other hand, we certainly were not going to allow any sailor of any color to be intimidated and perhaps stabbed by any soldiers or civilians of any color.

I picked the sailor up off the road, and he promptly dis-

appeared. So did two of the Negro soldiers. That left Rusty
and me with one stupid and scared Negro soldier glaring
at us with an open knife in his hand. That knife annoyed
me, and I tried quietly to talk him into giving it to me or
putting it away. He refused, and Rusty and I were just
about to take it away from him when I happened to notice
that everyone from the pub was standing there silently,
with others, making quite an audience. At that moment,
the soldier with the knife put it away and disappeared
through the crowd. Well, that was that, and at least this
English public had been kept from seeing and later talking
about a genuine, old-fashioned American race riot.

Then the woman who owned the pub—a rather lurid,
middle-aged redhead—came out from the crowd and
began screaming a lecture at me. She said that she had
seen everything, that we had persecuted a Negro, that she
had witnesses and was going to report us to the authorities,
that she wanted us to understand that we were in England,
not the United States, and so on and so on. I finally managed to get in a few words to protest that we hadn't persecuted anyone, and that we had simply stopped a fight
and had probably saved her license. I was so angry, for
the first time, that I wished I had socked the Negro and
lost her her license.

At that moment the MPs dashed up in a jeep, armed,
and wanted to know where the nigger with the knife was.
I told them that it was all over, and that he had disappeared. Then I told Charlie and Rusty that we had better
get back to our ship, and they agreed.

As we were leaving, an elderly English gentleman in
gaiters, a figure right out of a novel, came up and said to
me: "Son, I wish to apologize to you for the behavior of
that woman. Everyone here knows that she is a silly old
bitch. You stopped a fight and saved her license. I'm grate-

ful to you, and sorry for this scene." I said, "Thank you, Sir," and we were on our way. Rusty said: "Well, there are limeys and limeys, and that was a nice old boy."

Yet I felt that both Charlie and Rusty regretted that we had not simply socked that soldier and turned him over to the MPs, regardless. I was not at all sure that I had done the right thing. I was simply and literally nauseated by the whole problem. Back aboard, I overheard some Southern kid say to another: "Did you hear how Charlie Smart took on a fucking nigger with a knife?" All I could say was: "That's a lot of shit. I did no such thing." Then I heard the older of our two Negro mess attendants tell the much younger one that if he ever heard that he'd been seen with a white girl, he's cut his ears off.

Presently I got into another kind of trouble, right on board. Charlie Platt had been made a Chief Yeoman, and also Master-at-Arms, which is a disciplinary job in crew's quarters, under the Exec. One night when my boy Churgin had been working hard on the bridge, for many hours straight, and had finally been able to hit the sack, Platt came along when I was nearby and ordered Churgin to hit the deck and do some silly little job for which there were plenty of other boys available. Now Platt and I had always got along well, aboard and ashore, and he had always spoken to me before pushing any of my boys around, as is the custom between Chiefs. Perhaps I was tired myself. Perhaps I remembered suddenly what my first Captain had told me, that quartermasters outrank any other petty officers. Anyway, what I did was tell Churgin to stay in his sack and Platt to go away and play with his typewriter. What Platt could easily have done was to type out something on my jaw and crumple me like a piece of paper on the deck, but that would not have been advisable between Chiefs, and what he did was hardly more so. He put me and Churgin on report. Presently the Exec summoned us to his room and ate me out—a pleasure he must have long anticipated—but he did not bring us up to Mast. By this time I was desperately sick of that ship and her company—except for my few pals—and I wondered whether the albatross was hanging from my own neck.

21

On the evening of August 31 we were beached on the far side of Weymouth harbor, under the high, fortified rock called Portland Bill, and I was standing a combined signal and quartermaster watch alone on the deserted bridge. There had been no signaling, and I was furtively and happily reading *Romanticism and the Modern Ego,* by Jacques Barzun, who is one of my favorite writers, and who had been giving me a magnificent gift by writing to me, every month or so, a long, chatty letter full of ideas that, like Barzun's language, were manna to me in an LST.

Mr. Kleinhans came up the ladder and said: "Chief, are you in the habit of reading on watch?"

"Not often, Sir," I said, and closed the book.

Then he grinned, handed me a paper, and said, "Congratulations, Sir."

From the ship having the radio duty at the time he had received by messenger and had himself decoded the following from Washington: UPON ACCEPTANCE TEMPORARY APPOINTMENT AS LT (JG) DV—G USNR AND WHEN DIRECTED LT (JG) CHARLES ALLEN SMART DV—G USNR 364363 DETACHED X PROCEED PORT US X BUPERS ORIG X ARRIVAL FURTHER PROREP NEAREST NAVDIST FOR TEMPORARY DUTY PENDING FURASPERS.

All the officers were very cordial about this, and the Captain also wrung my hand but seemed disgruntled, which I took to be a compliment. Mr. Kleinhans told me, laughing, that my new number showed that I outranked every officer on board except the Captain. Charlie Platt, again a pal, claimed that he was the only enlisted man in history who had ever put an officer on report. In crew's quarters everyone wrung my hand and beat my back blue, but then I heard one mate say: "Oh, hell, as soon as he gets that fucking uniform, Charlie will be a son-of-a-bitch like all the others."

As soon as I could digest and credit this break, I was of course much relieved and very happy; to be going home so soon, to get a substantial pay raise for Peggy to a total of three hundred dollars a month, and finally, after two years and four months in the Navy, to get out of my peculiar position, difficult for me and everyone else. To have been an enlisted man was good in itself, especially on *456,* and also invaluable training for a commission, that most young officers lacked, and that incidentally had done a writer no harm at all, but it was high time for a change. As soon as I could get to Weymouth, I sent Peggy an exuberant cable, and this, I soon discovered, was a bad mistake.

The first catch was that nobody on board, or even in the office of the Eleventh Amphibious Force ashore, agreed on what should be done with me next. The Alnav, the printed order from Washington that included my commission, was missing on board—and that gave me a few, brief, dark suspicions, probably unjust—and nobody seemed to find it ashore either. Without it, apparently I could not take the oath and be detached—although this was later proved an error. Privately I wrote at once to Peggy's brother-in-law, Commander Henry C. Haskell, then in Washington, asking him to have someone find my Alnav and send it to me. Meanwhile, it was only agreed that I could take the medical examination and somewhere buy a uniform.

I was allowed to dash about in boats and jeeps, looking for a medical officer, and finally I found one in a sick bay somewhere ashore. He gave me a very careful examination, and then gave me one of the shocks of my life. He told me that I had a hernia, and that he could not possibly pass me for a commission. Oh, that God-damned hernia from New Orleans, which had bothered me a little in the past months, chiefly in the matter of fatigue, but to which, after that radio message, I had hardly given a thought. And oh, that stupid, premature cable to Peggy! For once I felt free to argue, and did, with no effect, while my heart sank. Then a medical warrant officer intervened —may his tribe increase!—stuck his finger up my crotch, argued strongly with the doctor, and finally convinced him. Gripping that signed paper, I got the hell out of there and back on board. There, since I couldn't get a uniform in Weymouth, I asked the Captain for a three-day liberty to go to London. The ship was being loaded for another trip to France, and he hesitated but finally grinned and said: "Why not, *Mr.* Smart?"

In the train, I had to stand all the way to London, but didn't mind that at all. Once more I was in the endless dusk and then total darkness, punctuated by bombs, of the heroic city, and once more I was with my English friends, the Wests, in Mitcham. They pampered me, crowed over my commission, and insisted that I get a haircut, while Wally's old mother insisted also on brushing and pressing my uniform, which, because I had never had a Chief's uniform, was still the gob suit of a Quartermaster First Class. The next day, Wally went with me to Selfridge's and fussed paternally over every detail of my uniform. He was much amused when, because of my long, narrow head, I had trouble getting a hat, and he said: "Ho, ho! The longest head in His Majesty's United States Ships!" I also bought Wally's wife some flowers and had mailed to Peggy a walking stick with a beautifully carved head of a cocker spaniel. When I had to leave the Wests again, I felt fairly sure that I'd have to return to London for transportation to the States.

I reached Weymouth in good time, only to find that *138* had not yet returned from France. At the amphibious command, I found that messages had been sent about me here and there, but no answer had been received. Everyone seemed to be fascinated and amused by the case of the man in the uniform of a Quartermaster First, actually a Chief, which he had been made after being commissioned a Lieutenant (jg); the man who had his officer's uniform in a paper box but could not put it on because he had not taken the oath and been detached from his ship, which had disappeared! I was ordered to sign in at HMS *Attack,* which was not a ship but a small, grim barracks on the Bill of Portland.

In that dismal limbo I spent most of a week. While I was there, I heard from Ralph Davis in *456* that she had gone into Leyte in the first wave and had taken some casualties, including the serious wounding of my friend Howard Gembler. After soaring, my morale hit a new low, and I was relieved only by my anger when a Chief succeeded in having me thrown out of the mess in that barracks because I was a commissioned officer, with a uniform in my gear. (I thought nobody had seen it.) I couldn't eat in the officers' mess either, so for several days I ate in the LSTs that came in, and in the Red Cross at Weymouth. Tiring of this life as a tramp or a Flying Dutchman, I complained to the commanding officer in Weymouth, who laughed, cursed, and then telephoned the

Attack to allow me to eat wherever I damned pleased, in whatever uniform I liked.

Just then *138* returned from the liberation of Jersey, which I should have liked to see, and I got a lot more mail, including, from Commander Haskell, the precious copy of my Alnav, with my appointment dated 29 February, 1944, when *138* had been on shakedown in Panama City, Florida. It was apparent then that if this Alnav had not somehow been lost, I might not have been one of "we happy few" or even returned to Europe at all. It was also clear enough that my commission had come to me, so long before, thanks only to my three different Captains in *456*, and also to the explosive old Commander of our squadron there in New Guinea.

When I was sent ashore with my precious Alnav, I was accompanied by the unfortunate Exec, who had had me on report a few nights before, and who was now eaten out by our Commander. It was quite a treatment, and when it had come to an end, and we had saluted, I stood there in my dungarees and white hat, holding the door for the Exec. He took it from me and said: "After you, *Sir!*"

On board, my orders were finally typed out and signed, and the Commander had ruled that I didn't have to take a new oath at all. The next problem was my pay, and in the disbursing office ashore, the Ensigns and yeomen went into a tailspin, because my record was so tangled. After an hour or so they told me that they couldn't figure it out, and that I'd have to get my pay in New York. I didn't like the sound of that, so I demanded my pay. In the middle of this scene a Commander came in and said: "Just what's the matter, son?" When I had shown him my papers and told him my story, he laughed aloud and said: "*Mr.* Smart, you will be paid every damned cent, here and now." And so I was. My take came to about six hundred dollars, and I hadn't had that much money in my jeans for years.

That night was my last aboard *138,* and it was darkened by something very brutal. Bill Kirby, a Motor Mac First, and a good one, had heard that afternoon that his ten-year-old son had been drowned. We were all much depressed, and we hoped that Bill could be sent home for a while, but doubted that anything so humane would happen. On the point of going home myself, I felt guilty and unfair. The albatross was still on board, if not on my neck.

The next morning, when I was putting on my new uniform and giving away my old pea jacket and the rest, Charlie English, Rusty Reisig, and other good pals dreamed up a joke. With them at my back to see the fun, I went to Mr. Kleinhans' room, jerked open the green curtain at the door, snapped on the light, and yelled: "Hit the deck!" Mr. Kleinhans leaped to his feet, dazed, grabbed his hat, saluted me, wrung my hand, and laughed with the rest of us. This parting was not like the one from *456,* but still, among those men and those officers, I had some stout mates and good friends, about whom I have wondered affectionately a good many times during the last twenty years.

After a few days ashore in Weymouth, including a lucky trip to Constable's Salisbury, I was sent back to London, with orders to join a ship at Helensburgh, Scotland, for passage to New York. At our Navy office in Grosvenor Square, I was told that this ship had been moved; I was told to return to that office daily, because they might be able to find me a place on a plane for New York. I had looked forward to seeing, if only for a few hours, a little corner of Scotland, but I now looked forward much more eagerly to flying home. Of course I saw the Wests, but I did not stay in their house, because at this time they had briefly at home, to their and my pleasure, their daughter from the Land Army, a son from school, and another son from the RAF. Instead, I looked up an American friend of my Paris days who was then living in luxury in London, and he very kindly put me up while I waited for transportation. My host was ill, so at night I roamed alone in the blackout.

One night in a pub I got to talking with an elderly British Major who was attached to General Eisenhower's office, and who was desperate because the General had ordered him to procure eighteen electric toasters for his staff. "It would be easier, my dear boy," he groaned, "to supply him with the crown jewels."

On another night I got into some trouble that still both humiliates and angers me a little. I was picked up by a couple of amusing fairies, to whom I made it clear that I neither shared nor scorned their peculiar pleasures. I risked their company for a few hours because I wanted to see some of the less respectable side of the heroic city at that time, and because they told me that they could show me some good Italian paintings hidden in the cellar of a dealer they knew. On both counts I was fully satisfied, so I foolishly invited them around to my host's house, and there we ate one egg each from his well-stocked refrigerator. The boys left quietly, but the next morning my host discovered about the eggs and invited me to leave his house! This was the first time this had ever happened to me, and I hope it will be the last. May West kindly procured three eggs for me from their farm, and I left these with my host's butler. While some men die in the surf and the hedgerows, and children and old people are buried in the rubble of their houses, other people worry about their eggs.

The next day, September 23, I was flown from London

to Shannon, and thence, in a NATS flying boat that had been a bomber, to Gander and New York. The plane was crowded with naval officers who outranked me and was also bitter cold, but I found the tail-gunner's seat, from which I could enjoy the moonlit sky and sea while remembering the time, seventeen years before, when George Stevens, Ogden Nash, and I doubtfully inspected Lindbergh's little plane a day or two before he took off. Flying fairly low over Plymouth, Massachusetts, I could almost pick out the house of Peggy's parents, in which we had been married. Do we all return, without planning to do so, and in odd circumstance, to places we have known? In putting his aircraft down in the boat basin at La Guardia, our pilot seemed almost to smash into a pier. Who is not and always in great danger?

It was good to get ashore, but after London, New York dazed me with its lights, crowds, luxuries, and quantities of young men not in uniform. My orders were delayed, so I was able to visit my mother on Long Island and my nephew at Choate. At my mother's school, I had to make a talk to the kids about D-Day, and that embarrassed me acutely; my only possible redemption was in urging them to study history *and* themselves, and then to try to do more to stop war than my generation and earlier ones had done. Peggy joined me in Manhattan, and I met her at Penn Station, which I am sorry to see torn down, because of such moments of delight that I have known there. After a few quite unreal days together in New York, we hurried to Oak Hill, where one of Peggy's sisters and four nieces were living a gallant new version of *Little Women*. This time I had thirty wonderful days, but of course they fled like so many hours, and the next thing I knew, Peggy and her family were pouring me on a night train to Norfolk.

My bizarre emergence "through the hawse-hole," my

sightseeing of war, and my breathing spell at Oak Hill were now over. I had learned that I'd probably be made the Executive Officer of an LST, and after criticizing many officers, I now had to "stand and deliver" the goods myself. It would obviously be the Pacific again, where men without women, little or big, were still being drowned, burned alive, and blown to bits, and where my incredible luck might not hold forever. Still, there was a very good chance that I'd see Peggy again, first, somewhere near that same damned old arctic inlet, Chesapeake Bay.

22

On that train there was a crowd of Ensigns and jg's, Middle Westerners, fresh from training at Fort Schuyler and elsewhere. All these clean, bright, young men were eager to get through their last period of training and board ships—as indeed I was also—but I felt about fifty years older than any of them. Among them there was a plump, genial Ensign named Hilmar G. Grimm, who taught history at Capital University in Columbus, and who kindly said that he hoped I'd be his Executive Officer. I said I hoped the same, but that seemed a very long shot.

This time we went to Camp Bradford, down the coast from Norfolk, and the quarters and food were good. Also, there were in that seething mass of men enough experienced officers, including mustangs, and experienced enlisted men, to make one feel that even the Amphibious Force might be able to finish its job in the Pacific. That this job was considered a big one by the powers above was made clear enough, tacitly, at a medical examination. Many of the naked officers in my line had been wounded, and I remember especially an ugly hole in a limping leg. My hernia was noted and brushed aside. All of us were passed quickly, evidently on orders from above. When they made us run through a brutal obstacle course daily, a number of us oldsters went to a medical officer and asked him whether they wanted us to operate ships or to incapacitate ourselves then and there. He relieved us from that folly at once.

As PCOs (prospective Commanding Officers) and PXOs (prospective Executive Officers) we went all day and every evening to classes in navigation, ship-handling, damage control, communications, gunnery, first aid, supplies and their records, personnel records, naval law, and many more, including those old movies on fire-fighting and venereal disease. All this had to be too hasty, brief, crowded, and theoretical, but most of us devoured all of it; because we had served in ships and we knew how ignorant we were, and we knew how useful the odd remembered trick or bit of information could be in a pinch. Rated men in their different departments and even junior officers, can scramble along, learning as they go, but Captains and Execs really ought to know almost everything. Later, I wished that I had had at least six months of that work instead of one, but obviously that was out of the question.

There were some odd and cheering punctuations of the work. At different times I ran into Silvester, Woodhall, Santarcangelo, and Shelton from *456*, and we had good reunions despite my uniform. Silver was ill, and the others were thin and yellow from atabrine, but the last three all wanted to get into my new ship. For my part, I surely wanted those stout and experienced sailors, but I was almost glad that I could not possibly get them, and for two reasons: supposing I got them and then they were killed or wounded, and supposing I got them and then found that I could not help favoring these old friends, or else bending over backward not to do so? As I had learned long before, the ship and her job are what count, and the Navy knows a great deal.

Then one afternoon, between classes or something, I

managed to sack in briefly and was wakened, to my horror, by a tall, distinguished-looking Commander, whose rank was bad enough, but he was also one of the best historians alive: Samuel Eliot Morison. He honored and thrilled me by asking me whether I wanted to work for him on his naval history, but he was about to go to the Mediterranean, and it was almost certain that I'd be irretrievably attached to a new ship's company before he returned. Again, I was almost but not quite glad that this could not be done, because I now felt somehow that I had to prove myself, if I could, as an Executive Officer, wholly involved, no mere observer, of an LST.

My next meetings were more important to me, as I knew at the time. Before we were given a crew, I was assigned to a Captain, and he and I were given seven Ensigns. The Captain, Lieutenant Leslie L. Hutchinson, was a dark, neat, tough-looking little man, about thirty years old, who had gone into the Navy before we entered the war and had served in a battleship and other ships, and later in a DE in the Mediterranean. This DE had been practically blown in two, and for his part in carrying on he had been given a Bronze Star. I learned about this from him only briefly, and much later, because he never bragged about anything. He had a wife to whom he was devoted, and one small child. He and I eyed each other with interest and reserve. I never did know what he thought of me, but I decided then that although he probably ate steel tacks, with skimmed milk, for breakfast, he was also probably a very good seaman, and the latter was much more important.

Of the seven Ensigns, only one, the Engineering Officer, rangy, humorous, and reliable, a mustang named Mr. Haupt, had ever been to sea. The Communications Officer was none other than Mr. Grimm, from Columbus, after all, and he still looked good to me. The others, Messrs.

Harris, Cohen, Bump, Littlefield, and Mitchell, all looked terribly young and inexperienced. After a day or so, the Captain said of them to me: "My *God,* Smart! Well, the thing to do is to work their little asses off." I agreed, but I felt intuitively, even then, the pattern of the months to come. If this Captain was a Bligh, he knew much more than any of us and would never crack up, and he might be able to save us from foul-ups and messes. If I was relatively ignorant, and probably too much interested in the officers and enlisted men as men, and too soft on them, I might be able to save us from too much bitterness that could also ruin our job—as well, incidentally, as our days and nights. I knew more surely that as Exec I'd be as lonely as all Captains always are. I was this Captain's liege man, who had to get done precisely and promptly whatever he wanted done, without ever one hint of criticism of him, and also without ever becoming a pal of any of the other officers, who were more or less equals and could be more friendly among themselves. The reader will see how all this worked out, with at least as many errors by the Exec as by anyone else. As a part of this pattern, the Ensigns and I always addressed each other as "Mister." Beneath it, Jack Haupt, Hilmar Grimm, and some of the enlisted men became furtively my valued friends.

Presently the nine of us went off with the officers of several other crews, and one crew of enlisted trainees, in a training LST, which had more guns, better radar, better everything, but was still a ship I partly understood. We stood watches, fired all the different guns ourselves, handled lines, made drawings of the fire-lines and other features of the ship, listened to lectures by experienced officers, and even conned the ship. This was actually the first time I had done this last, although of course I had stood beside officers doing it under almost every condition.

Usually I got away with it well enough, but one time I
botched it. I was bringing that ship without a keel, in a
stiff breeze, alongside another LST at anchor, when I mis-
judged something, parted a bow cable, which whipped
back and might have killed someone, and finally had to be
rescued by the instructor. My Captain was right there, and
this botch may have kept him, later, from allowing me and
the Ensigns to get enough experience on the conn. What I
enjoyed most was learning some new wrinkles in navigation from a Lieutenant Albert Gallatin, an architect and
(yes) a descendant of the great Secretary of the Treasury
of that name who always opposed spending any money on
the Navy. On that cruise, my Captain won $135 playing
poker, I read *The Tempest,* and we all froze as usual on
Chesapeake Bay.

In those years, one of the Christmas angels was looking
after me. On December 20 we went ashore, and for the
third time I had the great good luck and delight of spending Christmas with Peggy, this time in Washington with
our old friends Bill and Helen Crosby. Bill was now a
Colonel, and I was glad that he and his lady could take
us to cocktail parties and elsewhere in that city without my
embarrassing anyone with my old gob suit. At this time,
we were all depressed by the news of the Battle of the
Bulge. On the way back to Camp Bradford, I had to wait
three hours for a train from Washington, take one to
Petersburg, which took all night, and at dawn, over glare
ice, dash forty miles in a taxicab, with six other officers,
arriving to salute my Captain, at morning muster, precisely at 0700.

Later Peggy came down to a hotel at Virginia Beach,
and alone there together on January 1, we celebrated our
tenth wedding anniversary by drinking a bottle of champagne handsomely given us by friends with Ohio connec-

tions, Commander and Mrs. Forrest Wells. It was at this time that Peggy first met my Captain's charming young wife, who was ill, and whom Peggy was able to help a little, as she also did later. Peggy never did anything like that with an ulterior motive, but this kindness was appreciated by the Captain and his wife, and it probably helped save me from some very rough chewings-out later.

At this time, all was by no means liberty and champagne. We got more than a hundred of our enlisted men, and although they were still bunked and fed by the camp, it was now my job, with the help of the commissioned and petty officers, to keep track of them all, and to organize them into a ship's company by divisions (deck, engineers, bridge, etc.) into three sections for watch-standing, with each division represented in each section; and for the numerous different drills, involving parts or all of the ship's company. This complex game of the "Watch, Quarter, and Station Bill" involved *men,* not chessmen, who kept leaving (for illness or whatnot) and being replaced, and it had to be kept completely up to date and functional at all times. In general, and in theory, the Exec has to watch and operate the whole ship, through the officers, while the Captain has to watch the Exec and other officers, deal with other ships and all superiors, and take full responsibility. In this case, my Captain knew more than I did about everything except perhaps navigation, signals, and morale, and he was an active and invaluable help, as well as scourge, to all of us. Much later, on board, this went so far that orders began to get mixed up, and the authority of the officers, including myself, began to be undermined; but when I politely called these facts to his attention, the Captain promptly accepted the normal pattern, while demanding more severity on my part. This was his first command, and his anxiety to do a good job hardened his shell and roughened his tongue. With a few exceptions that gave us endless trouble, the officers and men seemed to me an average draw, or better, for the LSTs. When we took them all out in another training LST, and these men, few of whom were softies, began to become bitter and silent toward the Captain and of course myself, who had to shovel it out, I thought: Oh, my God, here we go again, and I wonder how long I can take it.

I thought the same thing again when some innocent Ensign appeared, grinning, with a copy of my *R.F.D.*, and in that way the Captain discovered I was a writer. All he had to say about that, with a steely grin, was that his wife had literary talent and that he almost regretted it, because "all writers are crazy as hell." "Certainly, Captain," I said, repeating my feeble joke almost three years later, "it's inevitable: an occupational disease." "Well, Smart," he said, "in my ship, you'd better take care to avoid it." "I intend to, Captain," I said.

23

When we returned to Camp Bradford, about January 16, the Captain learned that his wife was again very ill, there alone at Virginia Beach, so far from their home in Kansas. Luckily he obtained leave to stay with her for a while, but that left me in charge of the whole crew when we went through final inspections and entrained for Chicago. Until the Captain joined us there, and indeed until the end of this story, I was as busy with all kinds of administrative crises and detail—much of which was new to me—as a juggler with an itch. The Navy provides amazing foresight and support for a ship's company, as well as severe and unceasing pressure; sudden, violent, and often inexplicable demands; and a shower of paperwork, much of which seems a silly, exasperating waste of time and energy.

In Chicago, at first, all enlisted men were quartered on a long pier extending into the lake, while the officers were assigned rooms in a small hotel near the pier. I was kept dashing between the pier, the Navy office elsewhere, and the shipyard at Seneca, Illinois, where our new ship was nearing completion. Later, I had to take the crew to Great Lakes for more gunnery practice from the shore, and it was very odd to go back there as an officer with a crew. We stuck to as much liberty and practical training as we could get, and we did *not* parade and sing "Anchors Aweigh." In the midst of all this rushing about, the wives (including Peggy) and girlfriends of a number of our officers and men appeared in Chicago, and somehow we got rooms for all of them. For me, all this anxious and harassing hullaballoo was punctuated by some odd little experiences.

For example, one evening Peggy and I opened some mail together, and I found letters to me, about my *Wild Geese,* a book of cracker-barrel philosophy, from George Santayana in Rome and from Aldous Huxley in California. I felt immensely flattered by hearing from these great men about any book of mine, but I didn't quite believe that those letters were real. What connection could there be between those men and their worlds and me and my world at that time? Their comments, too, were almost comically contradictory. Mr. Huxley approved heartily of most of my social and other ideas, but deplored my "shyness about God." Mr. Santayana approved of my metaphysics (largely his own), but deplored all my social ideas. It seemed to me that his luminous intellect had become detached, to the point of callousness, from humanity in agony. I wanted to keep both my skepticism and my animal warmth and faith, if I could, while shoving the armed passengers of one ugly little ship down the throat of the Japs and getting my own boys safely home.

On another evening, Peggy and I encountered "philosophy" on a lower but still interesting level. We were dining by ourselves in a fancy restaurant when a corpulent old lady in much gauze approached us and offered to read my palm for a dollar. Considering my immediate future, Peggy's presence, and the fact that once in Paris Bravig Imbs had read my palms with incredible accuracy, I was hesitant, but Peggy insisted. The old lady told me that I was going to make many trips into Latin America and write about someone of another race. We laughed, because

I was not at that time interested in Latin America or other races. All I wanted was to become psychic with accuracy when we had to run too long on dead reckoning! Years later, we lived much in Mexico and I wrote a biography of Benito Juárez, a full-blooded Zapotec Indian.

The most moving event of that time in Chicago happened suddenly one afternoon. Leaving the hotel, Peggy and I encountered Mr. Haupt and his girl and Mr. Bump, our Gunnery Officer, and his wife. Mr. Haupt stopped us, told us quite casually that he and his girl had a date with a minister, in half an hour, to get married, and asked all four of us whether we'd be so kind as to stand up with them as witnesses. We all said that we'd be delighted and honored, so we piled into cabs and went off to a church in a skyscraper. Both Mr. Haupt and his bride seemed very mature, but to see these two good young people being married in that place, among strangers, so far from home, with the bridegroom about to go overseas, made me unutterably sad. Afterward, we six returned to our hotel, where I rounded up some other officers and their women for champagne in the wretched little bar, before the bride and bridegroom went out alone to dinner. I even managed to browbeat the hotel chef into giving me one small box of rice, scarce at the time, but necessary as a fertility symbol. I divided it up and we all threw it over them as they left the hotel.

Finally there came another ceremony not without its own emotions. On February 1, all our officers and those wives present, with myself acting for the Captain, went down to Seneca to see the launching of United States Ship *LST 1122*. The Chicago Bridge and Iron Company was building LSTs on an assembly line, on steel tracks, broadside to the Illinois River, and incredibly, they were almost finishing and actually launching one ship a week. Also, the

company was doing the launching up brown, complete
with sponsor, bottle of champagne smashed against the
bow, chaplain, band, luncheon, and cocktail party afterward for the officers and their wives. It was not entirely
gay, because our sponsor had lost a son in the Pacific, and
because the only thing certain about that ship and her
company was that they would never return to Seneca,
Illinois.

During that last hectic week in Chicago, the Captain appeared with his wife, whose health had temporarily improved. She was a lovely young thing, openly and properly
proud of her Captain, and the four of us had a good dinner
together, but the relation between the Captain and me had
to be tested and deepened by much more than that. About
February 6 or 7, we took the entire crew, minus the invalids and the AOL's, down to Seneca, joined the ferry
crew aboard, and shoved off. I had told the men that as
far as I was concerned, anyone who wanted to go AOL
at this point—and thence to a court-martial and a naval
or federal prison—instead of overseas with us, could do so
freely, because we didn't want to be bothered with any
neurotics or little shits on board. I think we lost one or
two, very well. It was not a bad parting from our women
in Chicago, because many planned to rejoin us, after
shakedown, in New Orleans. Everyone made appropriate
remarks on this subject to our bridegroom, Mr. Haupt.

It was very cold and dark, and part of the time we had
to follow an icebreaker. This time, the Captain, the other
officers, and I had little time to view the scenery, because
we were inundated with paperwork from Washington, in-
ventories, and such drills as we could manage without
sound-powered phones, not yet installed. When we saw
him, Ol' Man River looked much the same as a year or a
hundred years before. The Captain made Mr. Mitchell

Acting Chaplain, and although that nineteen-year-old told me that he had not been often in church since Sunday School, he led a service very well. Afterward, Harold Apple, our excellent Pharmacist's Mate, although himself very religious, found it advisable to call on science also by giving a lecture on venereal disease. While this was going on, I found a surreptitious poker game and confiscated a considerable pot for the ship's welfare fund. The almost-winner murmured, with a cheerful grin, "Fucked on Sunday, by Christ."

In New Orleans, we had the inevitable hectic week of workmen and inspecting officers on board, loading stores and ammunition, moving the ship—which I had to do once by myself—drunks from liberty parties, boat troubles, and all the rest of it. On Valentine's Day we were formally commissioned, complete with chaplain, band, and the works, but what struck me was that when it was my turn to bellow "Chief Boatswain's Mate, set the watch!" we had at that time, in the deck gang, only one rated man, a Coxswain. At the end of that mad week, we went to Mobile to go into drydock and get our bronze propellers. On the way, on the bridge, I found myself a bit rusty in navigation, but adequate, and there the Captain and I seemed to work together pretty well. It was fine to be at sea again, in our own ship, but after Mobile we faced again Panama City, Florida, and the necessary ordeal and nightmare of shakedown.

This time our Captain knew very well what he was doing, but the pressure from the shore command—reports, inspections, reprimands all the time—was even greater, and with this pressure from above and great inexperience below, he became a demon. There were no major goofs by the ship's company as a whole, but I'll never forget a dangerous little one I pulled myself. I had Mr. Haupt and a gang down in the after steering compartment, with flash-lights only (assuming all electric power had gone), to show them how to rig and unrig for hand steering. One impor-tant detail was not to put on the electric power before the windlass had been detached, because the handle of the windlass could kill a man. Without looking back first at the windlass, I said: "So *never* do this!" and threw the switch. The handle hit Mr. Haupt on the head and knocked him cold. We picked him up and revived him, I felt like a bloody fool, Mr. Haupt took it with extreme good nature, and the lesson, at least, was very effective.

One night, for ten hours straight, in a heavy fog out in the Gulf, we had tactical maneuvers in a formation of maybe six ships. The Captain, conning the ship, could see nothing, and while the Commander, in another ship, changed the courses, formations, and speeds every few minutes, by radio, our Captain had to rely on the data I shouted up to him from the radar and my maneuvering board in the chartroom. Our boy on the radar was inex-perienced, I was unused to the maneuvering board myself, and the men in the other ships couldn't have been much better. Remembering that ramming in the English Chan-nel, I was sweating ice water, and the Captain must have been doing the same, but Pallas Athena (or something) saved us all.

Our fortnight's nightmare ended with an extra-thorough cleaning of the whole ship, followed by a formal inspection and "battle problem" conducted by higher officers who came aboard. On the bridge, they would state a situation, such as "Bow door dogs have parted" or "All phones out" or "Fire on the forward tank deck" or "Rammed on the port bow and such and such compartments flooded," or a combination of these, and then see how we all responded to it. When I was down below, directing the shift to hand steering (without knocking anyone cold), I was summoned to the bridge and told the Captain had been killed. There he was, of course, watching me with a wicked grin. I checked up on everything—course, speed, tactical situation, damage aboard, guns, and so on—and tried to respond accordingly, but I forgot to change the speed cones on the yardarms to warn the other ships. When this little game was over, all I could hope was that *1122,* like *456* and *138,* would arrive in action only *after* the worst situations. Exhausted and relieved, we were then sent back to New Orleans alone.

Of course we had not known, and could not in any case tell anyone, just when this would happen, so that eight or ten wives, including Mrs. Smart and Mrs. Grimm, who had come down together, and Mrs. Haupt, arrived in New Orleans two or three days before we did. Peggy was older than any of them, and she had been through all this twice before. She helped them get rooms and pass the time, and she told them, with whatever conviction she could muster, that like bad pennies, we'd all return. She didn't give a hoot whether they were married to officers or enlisted men, and after we did arrive, she helped greatly by meeting at the railroad station the bewildered young wives (one a bride just over from England) of men I simply had to keep working on board. In general, in the months that followed, the officers and men of *1122* obeyed me cheerfully, quickly, and with all the skill they had, and this fact I attribute chiefly to Peggy's shrewd and imaginative kindness to their women.

It was during this hectic time in New Orleans that Mr. Grimm and I faced an odd job that was quite new to both of us. One of our AOL's in Chicago had turned himself in just after we left, claiming that he had missed a train or something, and he had been shipped to New Orleans to

join us there. With him there came an order to give him a
summary court-martial, on board. Because the Captain
had to review the case afterward, I had to serve as senior
member of a court of three, the others being Messrs. Haupt
and Bump, while Mr. Grimm had to serve as Recorder,
an odd combination of both prosecutor and secretary. I
raised the question of whether we had jurisdiction, considering the fact that the offense had occurred before we
had been formally commissioned as a ship, but a legal
officer ashore insisted that we had to go ahead with it. The
culprit, a good lad but stupid, pleaded guilty in advance
to the charges and specifications, so we didn't have to find
a legal officer to defend him, but this didn't please us
much, because the penalties would now be automatic and
severe, and although the Captain could halve them afterwards, we were not sure he would, and we were not allowed to discuss the case with him. All he could do at this
point was to warn us to follow the book, *Naval Courts and
Boards,* to the letter, so that he would not be humiliated
later by a reversal by higher authority. Mr. Grimm and I,
with a yeoman, boned up on that difficult book all one
night. When the time came, we had to take over the cabin
in dress blues, with an armed guard at the door, and with
Baker (no smoking on board) at the yardarm. The proceedings would have been funny except for the penalties;
but also, we wanted to preserve the dignity of any court
under our flag. We came near comedy only when Mr.
Grimm's needle got stuck while he was reading a long,
unintelligible legal statement, and we began hearing the
same damned thing twice. To our great relief, the Captain
did halve the penalties, which were then only some days
in the brig on bread and water and a considerable fine. We
made the record as impeccable as we could, but weeks
later, somewhere in the Pacific, we received from the Com-

mander a caustic rejection of the whole proceedings, on the grounds that we had no jurisdiction (for the reason I had surmised) and that our record had some commas misplaced. The Captain was not pleased. Then, according to the book, I had to read the Commander's rejection to the whole ship's company at morning muster on the weather deck. Afterward, the lad in question came to me and said that he had heard his name mentioned but had not understood one other word. I explained what had happened and told him he would get the fine back at next payday. "But Mr. Smart, Sir," he said, "I was guilty, I admitted it, and I didn't see anything unfair about any of it."

Despite a lot of hard work, by day and often by night as well, and a number of the usual minor crises and improvisations involved in getting a ship and her company ready for sea, we had some good evenings with our women in that ancient and fascinating city. When we were ordered to take the ship to Gulfport, Mississippi, for some final jobs, our women, including now the Captain's wife, went there by bus. Gulfport was a dull place, but every hour counted. On our last night ashore, March 22, I was delayed several hours by my successful effort to get one of our hundred-odd naval passengers, bound for the Canal Zone with us, released by the Shore Patrol, so that he would not lose his outfit. He had not done anything, but he had seen an instance of sodomy involving an officer, and was being held as a witness. When I arrived finally at the hotel, about 2200, Peggy was not critical. The other officers and their wives, except for the Captain and his wife, were in the same little hotel, and we had to take a boat to be on board at 0600. We had an alarm clock, as usual, and none of the others did, so I agreed to knock on their doors in the morning. When I did so, the answers through the doors might have been those to Death himself, and that group of men and women walking together down to the boat might have been walking down to the River Styx. Peggy and I weren't exactly singing, but hell, we had been through this for nearly three years, and you do get a bit tougher.

As soon as we got aboard, Mr. Haupt and I were absorbed in a problem of getting the ship to the right trim before the Captain came aboard, and I had to instruct the passengers and square them away. All this helped to keep us from staring ashore and thinking before we got under way, alone, at 1516 that afternoon. The other officers and men had jobs too, you may be sure.

24

It took us a week to make the fifteen hundred miles or so from Gulfport to Colón. The first few days were cloudy, and I was worried about the Gulf currents—and rightly so, because when I finally got a fix I discovered we were headed for the western tip of Cuba instead of the center of the channel off Yucatán. The Captain and I were working together on the navigation; he was good, and we got along well on that job. I had no regular watches, but I was also running the watches and constant drills, setting up a training program with Mr. Grimm, and so on. I got into the useful habit of wandering all over the ship, at all hours of the day and night, to check up on everything I could understand—and my understanding of everything but the engines and guns was increasing steadily. When the sky cleared, the air became warm, and the sea turned a brilliant blue, we all shook off the gloom of Gulfport, which was good, but unfortunately the less experienced officers and men seemed to be slipping into the odd illusion that we were on some kind of Caribbean pleasure cruise. We had an unusual amount of trouble with the deck division, and I'd have given more than a finger for Chief Shelton of *456*. The Captain and I took care to disabuse, or abuse, everyone on board, but he went further than that, even in the wardroom, where the climate became silent and bitter. I reminded myself and others that the Captain's wife was very ill; and for my own peace of mind I tried to ignore all that and concentrate on my many jobs, on the funnier little human details, and on the beauty of the always changing sea and skies. But I did not succeed very well.

At Colón I had a lot of work, with liberty parties, charts, stores, and this and that, including Apple's very proper concern, in that port especially, about prophylactics! We had to wait two days there to enter the Canal, and the Captain and I did have a somber drink together at an officer's club, discussing our shared worries. In the mail that reached us at Colón there came to me an icy breeze that touched my heart; the news of the deaths of an old friend at Choate, of two very promising young men in action (the sons of my friends Bob Haas and Dorothy Canfield Fisher), and of the disappearance of Paul Steel, a young friend and neighbor at home, who was just the kind of son that under other conditions I'd have liked to have myself. Paul, the pilot of a bomber over Japan, was "missing," and when I heard this news, and for months afterwards, I nursed the daydream that he had been picked up by the Japs, would be liberated, and would return in my ship— but even then I knew better. The only lights that counted were going out, while I, an old crock who had had my share of life, was still piddling along in comparative safety and already feeling too tired to look forward to being much good after the war. I was glad when we got rid of our naval passengers, all bound for shore duties in the Canal Zone, and took aboard a lot of armed soldiers who looked as though they could teach the Japs something about starting wars. There was always some relief from such thoughts, and when I had instructed these soldiers about their life and duties on board, the Staff Sergeant who was alone in their immediate command stepped forward there on the weather deck, saluted me, and said: "Sir, I'm sorry, but not one of us understands this Navy lingo at all." We finally moved through the majestic and fascinating Canal, with a good, loquacious pilot from Brooklyn and with good line-handlers in the locks, and took our departure for Pearl Harbor.

It was at the Canal that there began our long series of adventures and misadventures with animals for which I was in no small part responsible. Not long after we left Panama, several men appeared in my room to announce sheepishly that they had found several stowaways on board. These turned out to be a small cur named Pal, and two ducklings! Pal belonged to our very reliable old Signalman First, named Gerald Lackens, who ship-broke him and also made for him a small Mae West, in which he appeared and was secured on the bridge at general quarters. On the first of every month, when I announced promotions and demotions at morning quarters, I always included Pal, in one way or another, at the end. Some boys in the black gang owned the ducklings, and they solemnly swore to me that they would be kept invariably and superlatively clean in a small pen on the fantail.

When we passed within a hundred miles or so of an island called Bird Rock, many different birds stayed with us too long for the pleasure of the deck gang and of the gunners, who were trying to clean their guns and keep them so. One gull was especially persistent and dirty, and the gunners asked permission to shoot it, but I refused to allow that and told them, with surprisingly good effect, about the Ancient Mariner and his albatross. Then a clever signalman rigged a broom in such a way that when the gull settled down on a yardarm, as though on a john, he would catch a blow on his tail. The gull simply moved across to the other yardarm, but soon another signalman had a broom on that side—wham, squawk, wham, squawk —so finally the gull took off for Bird Rock, or wherever he lived.

On the evening of April 12, I was trying to get a star or two between clouds, from the signal bridge, and the Captain was trying the same from the bridge below. A tough radioman came up to me with tears in his eyes, which dumfounded me. He handed me a message from the Secretary of the Navy, saying that the President had died. For a minute or so, my stomach caved in, and I could not say or do anything. Then, remembering the Captain's bitter remarks about the President in the wardroom, I did something inexcusable. I went over to the rail of the signal bridge and called down: "Captain, here's a message that you alone, in this ship, are going to enjoy." He said nothing after he had read it, I heard nothing more about my impertinence, and he cooperated fully in what had to be done later. The rest of us, to a man, felt as though we had suffered a crushing defeat at sea or on land—or rather, worse than that, because somehow we had trusted the President to make some kind of sense out of all the horror, in the end. Our good Quartermaster, Reale, said to me grimly: "It makes you wonder what will come of it all." At that time we knew nothing about the new President, and of course it was months before we could feel his strength behind us. At that time, also, we knew that our men and ships were taking a mauling from the kamikaze attacks at Okinawa. Night fell without either the Captain's or my catching a star.

On April 15, at 0830, in accordance with an order from the Secretary of the Navy, but acting on our own ideas and resources, we held a ceremony in memory of President Roosevelt, with all hands not on watch mustered on the weather deck.* The Captain, who had been listening to the radio, first told about the circumstances of the President's death. Mitchell gave the Invocation. "Nearer My God to Thee" was sung by all hands. Mitchell then read two prayers from the burial service in the Book of Common Prayer, after which I read two selections from the President's speeches, on "The Four Freedoms" and "A World Civilization." The ship's company came to attention and stayed thus during five minutes of silence. Three volleys were fired by a squad, Mitchell pronounced the Benediction, and all hands sang the National Anthem. We were just one hundred eleven sailors, plus more than a hundred soldiers, in a small ship alone in the Pacific, grieving for a man we felt we sorely needed.

At about this time a sailor developed what Apple said was a badly inflamed appendix. The Captain decided against breaking the radio silence to send for an aircraft. Apple kept icepacks on the boy's appendix, fed him sulfa drugs, and finally fed him intravenously, which Apple had never done before, while I watched and sweated. The patient promptly improved, but then Mr. Harris developed an infection on his face that looked like erysipelas, which had killed my father. We now had six men awaiting medical examination and treatment at Pearl Harbor, assuming we found the place.

On the evening of April 22, a mountain peak on the island of Molokai appeared off our port bow exactly at the right time and place. Both the Captain and I were up most of the night as we ran through heavy showers in the Kawai Channel between Molokai and Oahu, and then at dawn

---

* I sent the program to Commander Morison, who later included it in his *History of United States Naval Operations in World War II,* Vol. 14, p. 232, and who sent the original to the library at Hyde Park. I wish that *USS LST 456 and USS LST 138* could also become, however oddly, a part of history.

past Diamond Head to the entrance of Pearl Harbor. We waited for hours for a pilot, and never got one, so finally the Captain took her in alone, with his usual skill. I was astonished by the narrowness of the channel into that huge harbor, which three and a half years before had been a death-trap. By this time the harbor was swarming with all kinds of craft under way, at anchor, moored, and in the great drydocks. We were moored among many other LSTs on the west side of Ford Island.

As always on coming into port, we were all plunged into many kinds of work different from those at sea. My first concern was always the crew, and for them what came first were mail, pay, liberty, and getting the invalids to hospital; and of course I had to make sure that the watches were set safely and justly. As Exec and navigator, I had to work my way through several large sacks of documents from the shore command and from Washington, making sure that each officer and leading petty officer got the ones that concerned his job, and that in the bales of rubbish, nothing important was lost or ignored. (Mr. Grimm, as Communications Officer, got sacks of documents that rivaled my own.) The other officers had to handle the food, water, fuel, ammunition, spare parts, and the repairs that could not be handled on board by our own men, but I had to make sure that all this was going forward, and sometimes I was able to help them with a few tricks of expediting and stealing that I had learned. Meanwhile, of course, there went on the endless job of repairing, cleaning and painting the ship, for our own safety and comfort and for inspecting parties.

After only a few hours of warning, one such party appeared, led by a four-striper. This time we had found in the crew a boatswain's mate who could use a pipe, so we did up the reception with as much style as we could manage. While the crew stood at rigid attention, in dress blues, on the weather decks, the Captain received the inspecting party at the gangway, and I waited at the head of the crew, just forward of the deck house. Just as the inspecting party appeared and I and all the other officers snapped into a hand salute, another little party appeared around the other side of the deck house. This new addition to naval ritual consisted of two fat white ducks, who waddled forward cheerfully, with their tails wagging and their yellow beaks lifted in joyous quacking.

While I stood there paralyzed, and my Captain came close to apoplexy, the inspecting four-striper stopped in his tracks, stared at the ducks for an interminable instant, and then burst into hearty laughter. Two bright sailors leaped from that end of the ranks, seized the ducks, and disappeared with them aft. The inspection proceeded, and we were saved from demolition less by the four-striper's sense of humor than by the fact that this time our ship was very clean from stem to stern and keel to truck. All the Captain ever said to me about this, and he said it with a grin for once, when a small piece of roast duck appeared on each officer's plate with a regular meal, was: "You God-damned farmer!"

Twice Mr. Grimm and I were sent to classes in ship-handling and the rules of the road at sea, and these were given around a glass-topped table, lighted from beneath, with model ships of various kinds that could be moved around on top of it. This was very interesting and important, but I wished we were getting more experience handling our own ship. She had to be moved fairly often, there in that crowded harbor, and I didn't always envy the Captain that job—as, for example, when a submarine suddenly surfaced uncomfortably close to our bow. The submarine skipper, or OD, was clearly in the wrong, I thought, but as his boat swept closely by us, he climbed out of his conning tower, shook his fist at our bridge, and shouted something inaudible that must have been vivid. Our Captain shook his own fist back and replied in kind.

Several times I managed to get ashore myself, and I enjoyed both the strange multiracial city of Honolulu and, from a bus to the north shore of Oahu and back, the volcanic crags with wisps of cloud around them, the bits of jungle, the scrubby cattle, the great fields of sugar cane and pineapples, and the vivid grays, greens, and reds of the island above the blue-greens of the sea. One evening I was royally entertained by Bill and Jayne Brown, old friends from my home town. Bill had been unable to get into the armed forces, and he was legal officer for the OPA in Hawaii. He and Jayne were also unwearied host and hostess, every weekend for years, to servicemen from Ohio. That night I disgraced myself by getting tight and into an argument with a Commander who lived above the Browns. As Bill drove me to a dock and boat the next morning, I wondered whether I was succumbing to my occupational disease.

One morning I was astonished by a signal by blinker from the shore command that went something like this: "Will Lieutenant Smart please get in touch with Commander Morison?" This was the first and last time that anyone in the Navy ever said *please* to me, and the Captain was even more astonished than I was. The result, a few days later, was one of the happiest days I had during the war. The Commander took me to lunch at his officers' mess, where we had a delicious soufflé and fine shop talk from my host on everything from the kamikaze attacks to medieval navigational instruments, including Chaucer's astrolabe, and from the position of Russia at the time to the migrations of the Pacific races. Afterward, he asked me whether I'd like to see Admiral Nimitz's office! When we were in that exalted place, then empty except for office furniture, maps and documents everywhere, the Commander asked me not really to examine anything there. "No danger, Sir," I said. "I had to study the plans for D-Day a few days in advance, and was scared stiff." When he asked me what the scuttlebutt was aboard *1122* about our next movements, I reported that we thought we might go in on the coast of China. The Commander merely smiled. Then he drove me in his jeep to call on a charming ninety-year-old gentleman named Frederick J. Lowrey, who was seated on the verandah of his house, set in a very fine tropical garden that made me long for Peggy. Mr. Lowrey was a retired merchant and the patriarch of a family that had been in Hawaii since 1879. He and his sons and grandsons had all gone to Harvard. We then drove over a spectacular mountain pass to the north shore, where we joined a beach and swimming party of highly civilized and interesting people of various races, including an anthropologist named Sir Peter Buck, who had fought at Gallipoli.

As soon as I was back aboard, I learned that we were going to leave next day, May 14, for parts of the Pacific considerably less civilized and peaceful. That night or the next morning, a Boatswain's Mate Second named Martin appeared from a receiving barracks ashore and begged me to sign him on. He had been kept ashore for a back injury. now almost cured, and he now needed an examination only about once a month, which I figured I might be able to get for him. He looked clean and competent, and I liked his eagerness to go to sea, westward. After looking into his case, I managed to arrange it, just in time. A couple of months later, under farcical and undignified circumstances characteristic of my life, he saved it.

25

During the next six weeks, until we finally headed for what looked like real business at Okinawa, we seemed to have nothing but misadventures, some comical and more of them exasperating and depressing, on an ocean that although so much vaster, reminded me of that of the *Odyssey*. Including even the Captain, we seemed to be sailors wandering we knew not where or why without even an Odysseus, working endlessly and foolishly without purpose or hope, even of returning home. The Cyclops, the Sirens, and all that did not seem to me more strange than millions of white and yellow men, in ships and planes that were microscopic on that sea, hunting each other to death. I kept thinking of the dead I knew and did not know. When I heard Apple mention God the Father, I could not even imagine any god like any father I or these men had known. In that ocean, any gods were terribly powerful and capricious, and if a Winged Victory alighted on our ugly little bow at the end, she would not be a splendid Woman, but haggard, emaciated, and in tears.

At Pearl Harbor, we took on another contingent of soldiers to be kept in line, and the tank deck was filled with loaded trucks. We then moved out in a convoy, and SOPA kept us busy day and night with signals and tactical maneuvers. All officers had a chance to conn the ship at last, and the Captain turned all navigation over to me. At one point, during maneuvers, one of Mr. Haupt's boys turned a wrong fuel valve, cut the fuel off the generators, cut all electric power off the ship, stopped the gyro compass, and froze the rudder at ten degrees left. When we arrived at Eniwetok, a shattered atoll crowded with ships, and had to anchor with speed and precision, the deck gang could not somehow let the anchor go. These were but two of many such episodes, and the Captain naturally grew savage.

However, in accordance with the pleasant custom at Eniwetok, the Captain allowed me to take ashore four of our officers, fifty-four sailors, forty-seven soldiers, a bat and softball, and two cans of beer per man. We beached inside the atoll, then walked through the palms and rubbish to the sea side, where there was a fine beach for swimming and enough room for a ball game in which the Army beat the Navy, 14–12. Soldiers, sailors, and even officers all got along fine together, and for those few blessed hours we were free men and equals once more.

This time, there were two catches. First, I returned to the ship in a boat in which Mr. Harris took the wheel and throttle and crowded into the cargo net ahead of a boat returning the Captain to the ship from elsewhere; so of course both Mr. Harris and I heard plenty about that. Then I discovered that I had hit my shin on live coral. This made a hole only the size of a dime, and I put iodine on it and forgot it until it ached like a boil, the pain seemed to come from the bone itself, and I found myself on my back in my sack, sweating, and a bit vague and delirious. Apple put on hot compresses and fed me sulfa drugs, and then the electricians voluntarily made a box with electric lights inside it, to enclose my leg and keep it hot all the time. I was touched by all this solicitude and by the Captain's taking over my jobs without complaint on the five-day run to Apra Harbor, Guam. However, during that vague, feverish time for me, I remember overhearing Apple telling someone I'd probably have to have my leg amputated in Guam, and my yelling: "To hell with *that* idea!" In Apra Harbor I was treated by a doctor, and while the Captain and other officers managed all our business ashore, I sat on the signal bridge with one leg in compresses in the sunlight and the other foot, rotten again with fungus, in a bucket of medicated water. From there, I could at least see or find out what was going on. It had almost pleased me to see how much everything had slackened off during my absence, but by this time both the Captain and I had seen enough of *that*.

Then one morning Apple wakened me about 0400 with the report that the same poor lad who had had appendicitis before, and who had *not* been operated on at Pearl Harbor, was having another very acute attack. I turned out a boat crew and got the boy ashore to a hospital, but in the process I discovered that the radio had not been manned since midnight! This was serious indeed, not only because the radio had to be manned *all* the time, but also because we were expecting orders to move at any time, by blinker or radio. This time I was furious, not only at the radiomen involved, who got Mast and deck court, but also, for the first and last time, at their officer, Mr. Grimm. For a few days I was in lonely despair, convinced that the Captain was right, and that all his officers, including myself, were a lot of incompetent creampuffs. The wardroom now fell totally and grimly silent, except at night, when the Captain was winning large sums of money from the Army officer passengers.

We now went on a four-day run to Ulithi, in convoy, with our Captain as SOPA, so that my own decisions about our positions were final, but all went well, and on that run we pulled one of our more comical goofs. We had received a collection of restricted intelligence reports that included, besides encouraging news about the bombings of Japan, a warning to look out for and report any fire balloons sighted; the Japs, with some little success, were sending them all the way across the Pacific to ignite the forests in the western United States. Well, that morning while I was working in the chartroom, the siren went off for general quarters. A sharp lookout had sighted a suspicious object, and Mr. Bump, the Gunnery Officer, then OD, had decided that it might be one of these balloons. He estimated it as having a diameter of some ten or fifteen feet, and being within range of our forties. It didn't look right to me, or evidently to the Captain, who had a bright idea and asked me where Venus was at the time. I looked it up in a hurry, and found that the golden little object with a visible diameter was indeed Venus, which I had never before seen by daylight. Poor Mr. Bump never heard the last of that one, and his only recourse was to point out that, as he claimed, one of our own cruisers had once actually opened fire on Venus. The odd dividend for me was that the moon was also visible on that clear morning, and I had the rare experience of getting, by daylight, a good three-line fix, from the sun, moon, and Venus.

Ulithi was a vast atoll, crowded with ships of all kinds, and we stayed there for two weeks, waiting for only Ernie King knew what. As usual, I was kept hopping with paperwork, on which I had the help of a good yeoman, Dick Hansen, and with personnel problems. The most vivid of these occurred when one of our soldier-passengers, a Puerto Rican who could not speak English, became desperately ill and Apple diagnosed the trouble—accurately, it turned out—as an attack of gallstones. In that huge atoll, the waves were at that time about six or eight feet high, but we had to risk lashing the patient to a stretcher and getting him down into a boat to take him to a hospital ship that was luckily at hand, a mile or so away. When we came alongside, an officer finally swung a boom and cables over the side, and when we saw that boy swung seventy feet into the air, we could only pray that we had secured the stretcher well.

In a large formation of LSTs, we had firing and other exercises outside the lagoon, and one day we had the job of releasing the red target balloons. For some reason we ran out of these before the exercise was finished, but at that desperate point Apple came up with the idea of inflating and releasing contraceptive rubbers. These expanded to about five feet in length, but were then almost colorless and invisible, so that we secured to them tails of rags, as on kites. After these had been shot down, some genial Commander made a signal: "What kind of balloons were those?" and when we told him, he said, "Congratulations."

Almost every night in that anchorage, our Captain either invited other LST Captains aboard to relieve them of their money at poker, or himself went to some other ship for the same purpose. One morning he returned aboard in a towering rage, with our three-man boat crew, but as passengers in a boat provided by his host. It appeared that during the night all three of our boys, ignoring well-known rules and explicit instructions, had gone aboard the other LST at the same time, for coffee and sandwiches, and while they were gone, the lines had parted and our boat had disappeared. Along with the boys, I caught plenty, and we were further humiliated when an officer and men from a merchant ship returned our boat, and the officer seized the opportunity to tell me that whenever the Navy got slack, we could always appeal for help from the merchant marine. I could provide hot acid on occasion, and our coxswain and his boys got their share of it that time.

The next morning, our Captain returned normally in our boat, but a few hours later I overheard part of an excited conversation that stopped suddenly when I appeared. I pumped these and other men, and soon I had the whole story, without much possibility of error or exaggeration. Once more our coxswain and his boys had left our boat empty and lost it. When they came on deck, they saw it drifting about fifty yards away, in a fairly heavy sea. Our coxswain promptly took off his shoes, dived overboard some twenty feet into the sea, and swam for his boat. Now an LCVP is 36 feet long and has a freeboard of at least three feet, so that the only way to climb aboard one, without help, even in flat water, is to get a hand and then a foot on the exhaust pipe. This our coxswain managed somehow to do, and then he got the motor started and took the boat back. The Captain had heard none of all this. I sent for that coxswain, and he sheepishly admitted the whole story, with no hint of pride in his feat. After my first salvo, the boy ventured to protest that I had told him that I'd kill him if he lost that boat again. I told him that I'd indeed rather kill him myself than write to his mother that her little boy had drowned himself because he had a brain that would fit into her thimble . . . and so on.

By this time we were all stir-crazy, the fumbles were fairly continuous, the Captain's invectives were the same, and most of the officers and men were silent, bitter, and sullen. The worst moment of all came when we were engaged in tactical maneuvers in formation outside the atoll, with the Captain on the conn, and at some critical moment the whistle didn't work. There was no ramming, but of course there could have been. Within the hearing of two officers and half a dozen enlisted men, the Captain said:

"If that happens again, I'll hang Haupt by his balls on a yardarm." Now Mr. Haupt and his men were probably the most reliable team on board; they alone had hardly ever made any mistakes, and this kind of thing, in a mechanism as complex as that ship, could have happened to anyone. Besides, Mr. Haupt was liked and respected by all hands. Presently some idiot repeated this unfortunate remark to him, and although he had a remarkable fund of patience and good humor, he now went about his work without a word, and with a white and haggard face, while the silence in the wardroom at meals became total.

Within a day or so, all the division officers appeared in my small room together, with their applications all made out for transfer. They told me that they had taken about all they thought they had to. My stomach was a piece of cold lead, because I felt that this proved at least as much my own failure as the Captain's. I thought it over for a while, and then I told these officers that the Captain could and probably would refuse to forward the applications, which would then make life in our ship up to that time look like a school picnic in a Hudson River Day Boat. I told them that we might soon be going into kamikaze attacks on Okinawa, which would not be funny even if we were working together as a good team, and that these applications would not make anyone in the ship—and there were hundreds of men besides ourselves, and a job to be done—any more efficient and safe; quite the contrary. I said that with their permission, I would tear up those applications there and then. After a short discussion, they all agreed, and I tore the papers up.

My relief was considerable, but not complete, because this unfortunate and dangerous affair seemed somehow unfinished, and my turbulent feelings are the only excuse I have—and a poor one it is—for what I did one afternoon and evening soon afterward, when I found I could get away from the ship. Mr. Haupt had some duty on board, but Mr. Grimm could get away, and I took him with me to the good officers' club that they had on shore at Ulithi. On the way across the rough lagoon in the boat, I said to our coxswain and his boys: "Look, Mr. Grimm and I are going to get plastered, and you are going to take care of the boat and us, and get us back on board safely. If I were running this Navy, you-all would have a chance to get plastered too, but I'm not, and you will just have to take it." "That's perfectly O.K., Mr. Smart," they said. "We're glad you have the chance, and you don't need to worry about a thing."

The club was an open shack, thatched with palm leaves, and the liquor was very good. We fraternized with another officer and his cocker spaniel, then Mr. Grimm and I talked, with increasing passion and lessening clarity, about our ship's troubles and four more interesting subjects: love of all kinds, art, politics, and religion. When we finally dragged ourselves away to our boat and our cheerfully waiting boys, the wind had stiffened, and the lagoon was even rougher, with waves maybe six feet high. When we came alongside our ship, even after lines had been passed to us, fore and aft, one had to stand on the bow of the boat, wait for the right moment, then leap for the lowest rung of the wildly swinging jacob's ladder. I caught it with one hand, swung a couple of times, laughing like a maniac, and finally clambered up the quarterdeck. Who was standing there, not amused, but the Captain? After I had saluted the ensign and Himself, I said: "Captain, would you mind stepping into the wardroom with me for a few minutes?" He did, and after I had cleared the wardroom of others, I told him drunkenly how I thought he was ruining the morale of his officers and men. He stared at me with a cold

grin and then told me to hit my sack and sleep it off. I was
glad to obey.

My awakening was not cheerful. A court-martial or a
bad fitness report for me? Increasing hell for all of us?
Apple volunteered a medicinal pick-up, and I went back
to work. The fact is that the Captain did not mention this
episode again, to me, or as far as I know, to anyone else,
and the next time he wrote fitness reports, must have given
me a very laudatory one. For this I was very grateful to
him. Except now and then, his general attitude on board
did not change very much. However, for a few days a tide
of suppressed merriment ran through that ship's company,
and this baffled me until someone told me that during my
impertinent and insubordinate but evidently vivid dis-
course, the ports of the wardroom had been open, and
just outside them, the OD, the gangway watch, and an increasing crowd of other sailors had been standing with
their ears buttoned open. Very well, but no young naval
officer reading these pages should conclude for one instant
that my behavior is to be imitated, even in a desperate
pinch.

On June 28 we finally got underway for Okinawa, with
our Captain as SOPA and OTC (Officer in Tactical Command) of a formation of sixteen ships of various kinds—
LSTs, Liberty ships, other odd merchant ships, and whatnot, plus three DE's as escorts. As Commodore, our Captain would have his hands full with his own work, and
would not have time to check up on my navigation, which
would govern the whole convoy. (Actually, he had not
been checking it for some time.) We knew that the kamikaze attacks had lessened, for the time being at least, and
that the Army and marines were about to secure the whole
island—which was happily in line with my personal policy
of arriving at such places just after the dirty work. How-

ever, as the Captain took care to point out to me, this was not enough to excuse the slighest slackness in any ship, least of all our own, or the slightest error by me as navigator.

As we left our anchorage and moved out through the channel, in order, we saw something that was rather heartening: one of our battleships—I don't know which one—dashing ahead of us at full speed. She quickly disappeared and, incidentally, that was the first and last time I saw a battleship under way in the Pacific. Those grand old dames served us well in the Battle of Leyte Gulf and elsewhere, but now they have all joined the *Constitution* in history. Convoys, at least as we knew them, may now be equally antique. Will major wars ever be grim curiosities of the past?

26

Every Executive Officer is required to read to his whole ship's company, once a month, the "Articles for the Government of the United States Navy," more familiarly known as "Rocks and Shoals." This time I omitted the obsolete passages of this ancient document and substituted the Gettysburg Address, after which I repeated the wise and hygienic statement of our first Captain in *456*, Lieutenant Perdue, that any man not frightened in action is either a clod or a liar, but that any man can be scared stiff and still go on and do his job. Actually, I had no fear that anyone in that crew would crack up, if we got into trouble.

Daily, of course, we ran through several drills, besides going to general quarters at dawn and dusk, and all these drills involved our restless soldier-passengers, as well as the crew. When the Captain criticized my drills as being "too tame and routine," I had a smokepot set off in a forward troop compartment, evacuated and far from any gasoline. These smokepots were the gadgets we heaved into the sea from our boats when we were at anchor, to supplement the smoke made by our smoke machine on the fantail, in making a smokescreen. The effect was very good, and the boys got the hoses down there in a hurry, but the smoke steadily increased instead of lessening, and when I hurried down there I found we had set fire to a mattress. Afterward, the Captain said: "Smart, you God-damned dream-boat, you don't have to go theatrical on me *now*, for God's sake."

All such matters were now marginal, in my mind, to my critical job of navigation for sixteen ships. All went went until July 3. We were going to approach our destination, a group of islands south of Okinawa called the Kerama Retto, the next day, and during the night of the third we had to make a sharp change of course to port, on a precise spot, at a precise time, with all ships without lights, of course, and we had to do this before another convoy was due to approach us from the starboard and fall in behind us on the new course. Since some of our ships did not have radios with which we could reach them directly without our breaking a larger radio silence, I had to know before darkness fell and the last signals could be made to them by flaghoist, exactly when we were going to make that radical change of course during the night. In other words, I had to know exactly where we were all the time, say within a mile, and exactly what speed we were making.

On both critical matters, I had disturbing doubts. The sky was slightly misty all day, just enough to worry me about the accuracy of my sun-sights. Furthermore, at that place and time, the sun's azimuth was changing very little all day, so that my sunlines, as I advanced one against the next, in accordance with our *estimated* speed, were much too parallel to give me good, sharp Xs on the plotting sheet. Worst of all, I was doubtful about the accuracy of the current chart for that place. We were being pushed somewhat from astern, but I did not know exactly how much to figure on, in relation to our speed as indicated by the rpm of our engines. I couldn't have told anyone just why I was doubtful, but I had long before learned to trust hunches like this that are often ignored by beginners, hunches that make navigation both more safe and more worrisome to the navigator and his Captain.

In those sixteen ships, there were surely many navigators who were more experienced than myself, and during the morning I hoped that when I asked them all for their noon positions, they would come to me as a cluster close enough together to reassure me about my own position, or to correct it. However, when their positions came to me by flag-hoist, they were more widely scattered than they had ever been, and gave me no reassurance or correction whatever. All I could do at dusk was hand down my own position as the law. All afternoon, I kept taking sun-sights without becoming any more confident in them. As the sun began to slide down the western sky and the time drew near for making the signal about change of course during the night, I decided to swallow my pride and explain the situation to the Captain. Much annoyed, he came down to the chart-room from his busy job on the conn, and studied the plotting sheet and my calculations. Finally he snorted and said: "Well, Smart, we'll just have to take your own word for it, and see how good you really are." With this he returned to the conn. I went over the whole problem for the twentieth time, and decided that we'd have to change course at say 0050 in the morning. Presently the Captain leaned out from the conn and called down to me on the bridge: "O.K., Smart, now's the time and what's the word?" I gave it to him, and within a few seconds this order was being spelled out in flags from our yardarms and was being acknowledged by all the other ships. Well, that was that—but not quite.

Naturally, I was crazy to catch my old friends the stars, and to my delight, as the sunlight failed, the sky and horizon became much clearer. I caught half a dozen stars, worked them out quickly but carefully, and got a fix in which I had absolute confidence. Now I knew exactly where we were, but I promptly discovered that that damned current had indeed pushed us faster than I had estimated, and slightly off our course. This meant that we had to change course slightly, and fairly soon, if we could, and that we should then arrive at the exact place for a radical change of course to port, to 291°T, at 2353 instead of 0050! I had been about an hour, and some nine miles off, and I had proved myself a somewhat incompetent fool, but if we could somehow get the word to all those other ships, our convoy and that other one would be much safer as we approached those islands.*

My first step was to summon Mr. Grimm, who (bless him!) worked out a scheme for getting the new word by local radio to all of the ships but two merchant vessels. We could only hope that when we changed course nearly an hour ahead of time, their OD's or Captains—perhaps having got the stars also, and done some thinking—would catch on in a hurry, and not ram anyone else, or be rammed. Next, I had to go to the cabin and report this situation. I found the Captain in his skivvy—shirt and shorts, and he stared at me with his hard, dark eyes and said simply: "God damn you, Smart. Get on up there, and I'll be right up." When he came into the chartroom he looked at my starfix and figures, then turned to Mr. Grimm, who was waiting there with all the answers ready, about radio. The Captain told him to give out the radio order as we had planned it, and to stay in the radio shack until relieved. We made the slight change of course without trouble, and then the Captain, the changing ODs, and I stayed on the bridge all night, without exchanging any

---

* These figures are from our log, now in the National Archives, which I checked to make sure. My memory had been astonishingly accurate, for me, but then, of course, this was an experience anyone would remember. It was very odd to read all those dry logs, many in my own handwriting, in that sacred place. Many pages had been removed by ONI, or someone. What endless dramas behind all those dry facts and figures!

light chitchat. At 2353 we changed course to 291°T, and then stared at all the other ships, and especially those two merchant ships who had not been informed, through our binoculars. After very short hesitation, those two caught on and changed course with the rest of us. Soon after, our radar man picked up the blips from that other convoy, which fell in astern of ours. My stomach began to calm down.

At dawn we made the correct landfall, and I began to take bearings and plot our course between those islands. The Captain said: "Smart, you have much more luck than brains" and I said: "I quite agree, Captain." (I still agree to that.) Those bright green islands were beautiful in the early morning light of July 4. This was part of Japan, which in *456* had seemed so many miles and years away. Brave men had died all over the Pacific, and a few days before in those very waters, to get us and our soldiers there, and it was not impossible that by daylight a few final kamikaze boys, having heard of us and that other convoy, would appear like thunderbolts from a clear sky. Of course every gun in our ship, and in that convoy, was manned, and scores of binoculars were searching the sky.

Meanwhile, Mr. Grimm and I kept taking bearings and checking the plot, up there on the conn, while the Captain drenched us, and especially me, with a virulence of comment that was new and extreme in my case. For a while, this seemed fair enough, considering my error of the evening before, and it pleased me to think that the other officers might well be thinking, with some justice: "Well, now Smart's getting it, too, at last, and may be able to understand us a bit better." However, I was extremely tired, my damned hernia and sore feet were bothering me, and above all, the Captain wouldn't even let me go below to get a cup of coffee and take a piss. Finally Reale, that good quartermaster and man, appeared furtively behind me with a bucket and a cup of coffee. The riding continued, and then, with astonishment, I heard myself saying: "Captain, if you don't like my work, all you have to do—" At that point I thought better of it, and held my tongue. I don't know how I was going to finish that sentence, perhaps with "give me a bad fitness report," or something worse. There followed, to coin a phrase, a pregnant silence, and then our work continued. We went into the crowded anchorage at Hagushi, and we let that anchor go on a dime—which, if I do say so, the Captain and I knew how to do. The curious fact is that from then on, for several nights and days, the Captain's sarcastic criticism of all of us was discontinued. He was a fine seaman, that man, doing a critical job, and as it turned out, he was even more tired than I was.

After the Captain had gone ashore for meetings and orders, we were sent down the coast to the harbor of Naha, which was small and dangerous because it was crowded with the hulks of sunken Japanese craft. The town itself was reduced to rubble, and the marines were camping around fires in the ruins. They had no comforts and were short of food, so they were catching or shooting the domestic animals of the natives, who had been moved to camps. Although we were not allowed to disembark our soldiers and their vehicles for two days, we allowed as many marines as we could to come on board for baths and for any food we could reasonably spare. All marines are accomplished thieves, and they stole almost everything that wasn't welded to the ship, but they had been doing our fighting for us, and whenever we could, we looked the other way. As the Captain might well have predicted, I carried this too far when I allowed our Chief Steward to trade a sack of sugar for a live pig—or rather, shoat—

which he swore to me he would keep completely out of
sight until it could be turned into fresh roast pork.

Finally we disembarked our passengers, cleared the tank
deck, and prepared to get off the beach and return to
our anchorage at Hagushi for further orders. The afternoon light was fading, the wind was freshening, and the
Captain was naturally very eager to get out of that dangerous harbor by daylight. I had the engines lighted off, set
the special sea detail, made all the required checks, and
reported to the Captain that we were ready to get under
way. At the very last moment there came up word from
the tank deck that they were having trouble with the ramp.
When I went down there to investigate, the bow doors were
still open and the ramp, bridging water, was still down on
the steep, sandy beach. The ramp of an LST is a large
box of steel, fifteen feet wide by twenty-three feet high,
and perhaps two feet thick, and it has a number of holes,
about a foot in diameter, on both the outer and inner sides.
From inside the ramp there came piercing squeals that
could have been heard in Tokyo, from that damned pig.
He must have escaped from his pen, been pursued down
the tank deck, and fallen or ducked down one of those
holes, into the ramp. A crowd of sailors and marines
surrounded the ramp, laughing, stabbing through the holes
with bayonets, and drawing pistols. I stopped all that, because if they killed the pig, we might not be able to get
the carcass out, the Captain might well order the ramp
raised regardless, and the stench would be there during
the weeks we might be under way. At this point, some
brave and ingenious sailor got my permission to go into the
water under the ramp, in hopes of catching the pig by a leg
through one of the holes on the under side. In a few minutes he came to the surface beside the ramp, with the
squealing pig firmly gripped by one leg. He heaved the

pig up on the sand, and it rapidly disappeared. Meanwhile a silence fell on that crowd, and as I looked behind me, I saw the Captain.

"*Mr.* Smart," he said, "are you a farmer *or* an Executive Officer, *is* this a ship, and IS *she ready to get under way?*"

"Yes, Sir," I said meekly, while the marines scuttled ashore and our boys raised the ramp and closed the bow doors.

Back at our anchorage, we were plunged into the usual jobs of cleaning the ship, taking on stores, and handling a mass of paperwork and administrative tangles. My most troubling problem was that of a sailor who seemed to me to be clearly suffering from manic-depression. He was a pathetic but dangerous nuisance to everyone and the hospitals ashore were packed with men wounded in action. When I finally found a psychiatrist in another ship, he was no help at all. Meanwhile there was a lot of scuttlebutt about the future of the war and of ourselves. It looked very much like an attack on Kyushu, which would be no picnic.

Several times, by day and night, we had alerts of air attacks, but saw no Jap aircraft or firing. I don't know yet what those were all about, because Admiral Morison says that the last kamikaze attack occurred on June 22. At 0328 on July 12, another alert made us go to general quarters and also make smoke, because we were anchored upwind of a great mass of ships. The smoke machine on the fantail began to pour it out at once, and the starboard boat got away promptly, to dump smokepots in the water upwind, but after the port boat was in the water, it unaccountably slipped aft, instead of going upwind off the bow. When I went aft to investigate, the smoke was so thick that you couldn't see your hand six inches in front of your face, but I stumbled about among the men and machines and found that the port boat had not been fully loaded with smokepots. She was under the stern, and the boys were blindly passing smokepots down to her. I helped, and as soon as they were all aboard the boat, I decided to go out in that boat, just for the hell of it. "Stand by with the boat. I'm coming down the line." "Here we are, Sir."

I went down the line to its end, then dropped, and I landed not in the boat but in the water. I couldn't even see the stern of the ship, and I could only just hear the boat's motor, without being able to determine its direction from myself. I had on my Mae West, which made swimming easy enough, despite my shoes, but instead of my helmet, I was wearing my peaked hat, and suddenly it occurred to me that if I lost that one hat, obtained with difficulty in London, I'd be in a pretty fix for inspections, morning quarters, and so on. While I was laughing madly at myself, I heard someone yell from the invisible fantail: "The Captain wants to know what's the matter!" Then I heard the boat's motor, and the coxswain yelling: "Nothing's the matter! We're on our way!" This boy, Martin, was the one I had signed on at Pearl Harbor. Then I heard him, still closer, saying in a loud stage whisper: "Mr. Smart, where are you?" "Here, here," I whispered back, still laughing. I swam for a while, and the boat seemed to be circling around me. Finally it loomed up beside me, and the boys, Martin and Hoag, grabbed me by the hand, the shirt, and the seat of the pants, and hauled me up into the boat. By this time, they were all laughing too. "Do you want to go back aboard, Sir?" "Hell no!" I gasped. "Let's get out there with these smokepots, fast!" After we had got well started upwind and off to port, I could just hear our Captain on his bull-horn: "Mr. Smart, report to the conn! Mr. Smart, report to the conn!" I decided that the smokepots were more important (and more fun), and nobody in that boat heard anything. When I finally reported to the conn, all the Captain said was: "You God-damned fool!"

Once I got ashore with our Captain, Mr. Grimm, and the Captain of another ship for a bit of hitchhiking and sightseeing. The whole scene was extremely desolate and depressing, except for the stolid resignation and even good cheer of the GIs, all stripped to the waist. I remember especially the lethal caves, the occasional smell of corpses, and picking up a few fine little dishes made by those specialists in beauty and in the deaths of their fellow men and of themselves. Against that background, I could not intellectually consider important the news that came from Peggy that my own beloved little cocker bitch, Jeannie, had been killed by an automobile right outside our garden. However. . . .

On July 14 we were ordered back to Naha, and there, the next day, we took on board a load of vehicles and embarked a large unit of marines, all combat veterans from the 6th Marine Division. Frankly, we were relieved to learn that we were going to transport them back to Guam, via Saipan, instead of into the next big attack, wherever that might be. That job was for heroes, and not for clowns like ourselves. (Of course we didn't have the dimmest notion about the experimental explosion, two days later in New Mexico, derived from the "metallurgical laboratory" under the stands at Stagg Field in Chicago.) Although the marine officers seemed, tacitly, to view our methods with surprise, they were an unusually congenial group. When my roommate, Lieutenant David V. Lourie, noticed on my desk a postcard reproduction of Chardin's *Card-Player,* that released from him a flood of good egghead talk that stopped only when our Captain was winning his money and that of his fellow officers.

While not running drills and trying to keep my enormous family in some kind of order, I was plotting, from radio messages, the location of a typhoon moving in our direction. At 0619 on July 19, when it was nearly upon us, we were ordered out of the anchorage in a formation of scores of ships. As I remember it, we went all the way around the north end of the island and out to sea to the east, where we stayed for three days, just moving around to keep our bows into the wind until the storm blew itself out. With the wind rising to a high-pitched whine—although it was logged at only thirty-six knots—our little ship with no keel slid up, down, and around the huge waves like a skiff or a chip of wood. In that kind of weather or less, from the conn of an LST you can see the whole ship bend like a whip. The Captain let me and other officers do a good deal of the conning, and I was glad we were getting the experience. Our passengers were seasick all over the place, and that tended to lessen the air of superiority with which the enlisted marines had come aboard and mingled with our sailors. Now and then I thought of *The Nigger of the Narcissus* and I doubted whether we, in a safer ship with diesel power, could have taken it as long and as nobly as Conrad's sailors. Finally that damned typhoon blew itself out, and when we were back at our anchorage, SOPA made a "well done" signal to all ships involved.

Meanwhile, an Alnav had come through that included me among the promotions, by seniority, not merit, to Lieutenant, senior grade. Apprehensively, because of my hernia, I looked for a doctor to give me the necessary medical examination, but when I found one, in a transport, he said: "Hell, if you can work out here, I'm not going to keep you from any promotion." In our boat with me I had taken a congenial marine, Captain E. J. Tutag, to see a friend of his in that transport, and that friend gave us a good drink. I also managed to buy some cigars to hand out when back aboard *1122,* but these didn't go very far. Captain Tutag kindly found, among his fellow marines, two pairs of silver bars for the collar of my shirt. It was all very pleasant as comradeship, but it gave me a queer turn when I heard someone suggest that I was now likely to get a command. I wrote to Peggy, truly enough, that I was exhausted and didn't give a damn about the promotion or anything else. So ended my trivial part in the Okinawa campaign, "not with a bang but a whimper."

27

On July 22, we got underway, in a formation of twenty-five ships, with three escorts, for Saipan, and that run took us six days, after which we moved quickly on to Apra Harbor, Guam, where we arrived on July 30. This run was easier on me because our Captain was not SOPA and my navigation was not, therefore, decisive. It was also easier, in a way, because our Captain, now exhausted, intensely nervous, and clearly ill, spent most of the time in his sack. Yet his condition worried me very much, because we had no doctor on board, Apple's diagnosis was uncertain, I trusted and needed this man as a Commanding Officer, and in spite of everything I had come to like him. However, my days and nights were so filled with navigation, tactical maneuvers, drills, and disciplinary problems that I didn't have much time left to worry about the Captain.

When we went into Apra Harbor, this problem presented itself in full force. We were ordered to beach in a certain place, between two other LSTs, and the Captain, who then had the conn, and who had beached the ship successfuly in scores of places, was clearly unable to make up his mind and go on in. He kept turning her around in circles, and while this was going on, I got a personal message by semaphore from Charlie Dunlop, an old Ohio friend who was in command of the armed guard of a

Liberty ship. I signaled that I'd see him later, and the Captain finally took her on in. We unloaded the tank deck and disembarked the marines who, on going ashore, somehow concealed the electric fans they had stolen from the crew's quarters. We were kept moving the ship all night, but I managed to visit Charlie Dunlop aboard his Liberty ship—in which he was teaching his gun crew history, geography, and mathematics!—and then to bring him back aboard *1122* with me for evening chow, which was interrupted by an aircraft alert.

The next day, the Captain was really sick, and had to stay in his sack. I sent one of the officers in a boat to find a doctor in some other ship, and then I went ashore in the other boat to speed our Supply Officer in getting some very necessary stores, including food and engine parts, and also to substitute for the Captain at a Captain's meeting at 0800. I was told to return at 1200, and that we'd get under way at 1600, and on that basis I arranged the boats and the stores parties. Back on board, I got a radio order changing the meeting to 1300 and the sailing to 1500, which would make it a very tight squeeze with the boats and stores. At the meeting, it was revealed that our Captain outranked the other two Captains in the unescorted convoy of three ships only. I was surprised and happy to learn that we were going all the way back to Pearl Harbor, but I was worried about our Captain and about my position if he could not carry on as SOPA. When the Commander asked about his health, I told him what little I knew—exhaustion, bad cold, low pulse, low blood pressure, subnormal temperature—and about my having sent for a doctor. The Commander and the other two skippers, the latter old Navy hands and friends of our Captain, assumed he would pull out of it and resume command, and I could only hope so.

I did what I could to speed the stores and the boats, then caught another boat and hurried back on board to see the Captain. I told him about our instructions for procedures underway, and he told me that the doctor had told him that he was suffering from exhaustion and possibly pneumonia, had ordered him to remain in his sack, and had instructed Apple about his care. Lying there in his sack, the Captain seemed to glare at me indifferently from about a mile away. "So she's all yours, Smart," he said, "and the hell with it." Thinking about the Captain's nice little wife, I checked with Apple, who seemed to have the situation as well in hand as it could be. It was now 1500, and from the bridge I could see the other two LSTs waiting for us outside the harbor, but our damned boats with their men and stores had not yet arrived. When they finally came, they had to be unloaded and then taken aboard, while I sweated.

We finally got underway at 1637, without having received an angry signal from the Commander ashore, and I made tracks for the narrow channel. There, when I was foolishly barging ahead at full speed, I got a shock: a few hundred yards ahead of us there surfaced, with no warning, a submarine. I stopped the engines, then reversed them, and pulled as far off to starboard as I could. Just as had happened in Pearl Harbor, the submarine's Captain or OD appeared on the conn and shook his fist at me, and I replied in kind. Mr. Haupt told me later that the sudden stop and reversal had given him and his black gang quite a turn.

We took our place at the head of the other two ships, I gave them their orders—wondering what they would think if they knew who was giving them—we moved down the coast, and that evening we took our departure for Pearl Harbor. Fate had kept me from becoming a commando on the French coast only to make me responsible for leading three ships safely across thirty-five hundred miles of an ocean for which I still felt great respect and in which the enemy was still active. We did not know, of course, that at that very time some nine hundred men of the *Indianapolis* were dying in that quiet sea, not very far to our west, partly from Japanese skill and partly from the carelessness of American officers ashore at her destination.

The wardroom was now as merry as a crew's quarters could be, but I tightened up on all the cleaning, drills, and watches, and had Mr. Grimm run flaghoist drills between the three ships, which he did very smartly. There were the usual signals between ships about station-keeping, general quarters, exchanging movie films by lines, positions at sea, and so on. The traffic was surprisingly heavy for that remote area, and by day and night the ODs and I had our share of bad moments, always remembering the stern injunction of the rules of the road at sea that the ship with the right of way must hold course and speed until the last minute of safety.

At least once a day I visited the Captain in the cabin and checked on Apple's care of him, which seemed admirable. His condition did not change much, and when, every other day or so, he dressed and came out on deck or climbed painfully up to the conn, he was either very nervous and critical or could hardly speak. I wished heartily that I could double or triple the speed of our three fat old ladies and get that man into hospital at Pearl Harbor. When he became a little stronger, he gave Mr. Grimm some stiff daily lessons in navigation, which was an excellent idea in case he, the Captain, as he hoped, should be relieved of command. I tried to keep that possibility firmly out of my mind for the time being.

We had some misty or cloudy weather, but only once, on August 5, did our position at sea really bother me. We were coming near Eniwetok, which has its share of reefs, I had not been able to get any stars the night before, and at dawn I didn't do much better. When I got the 0800 positions of the other ships, all three of us were much too far apart for comfort, and I could not then get any reliable sunlines. If a latitude I had got at dawn from Polaris was correct, we had soon to make a change of course that was certainly not indicated by the positions at which the navigators of the other two ships thought we were. However, the decision was mine alone, and I ordered the change of course. Presently radar and then a visual sight of the island fully confirmed my decision; if I had trusted the others, instead of my own "iron string," we might well have got into trouble.

On August 6 we heard about Hiroshima, and then soon about Nagasaki, the entry of Russia into the war against Japan, and the peace negotiations. Of course we were all excited, keenly interested, and considerably baffled. The Captain remained dressed and camped himself on the radio and, as I remember it, he saw the tremendous significance of those bombs more clearly than the rest of us did. He actually talked about finding a remote island and moving to it, after the war. I must admit also that I felt very little compunction about the deaths of the Jap women and babies, who had in any case, like the German civilians, been pulverized by our more conventional bombings. Just which people supported or tolerated the governments that had started this war? Admiral Morison has since argued very effectively, with evidence, that the Japs were by no means beaten before the bomb, that it had to be used just as it was used, and that it saved a great many American *and* Japanese lives. The most effective weapons will always be used by any nation that has them; disarmament alone will never be effective; and the real problem is the federation of nations, which will not be achieved—if ever —until the better people in all nations seize and retain democratic power.

At that time we all distrusted the Russians, and we all favored keeping and using the Emperor of Japan. "Sure," said one sailor, "keep and use the silly bastard. They can shoot him anytime." Crossing the dateline, we had two August tenths, and also some heavy swells with a brisk wind. The ship bucked like a bronco, shivered, shook, rolled, pitched, and did handsprings. The sky was almost always cloudy, so that for a while Mr. Grimm and I were more concerned about our position than that of the Emperor.

On August 14 I was getting the meridian altitude at local apparent noon, 115620, and then the positions of the other ships, when we received the President's announcement of the victorious end of the war and also a timely message from Secretary Forrestal, sending congratulations and requesting discipline and patience. (*Requesting*: he was still a civilian.) After chow, I ordered all three ships to test pyrotechnic ammunition, which was the only form of celebration anyone could think of. Of course in the bright sunlight, the Very pistol lights, rockets, and so on were not much good, but the colored smokes were good, and in any case I did not dare delay this show until night, because we were now fairly close to Hawaii, and I felt sure that some destroyer or aircraft would spot us and come dashing out to find out what was going on, with unpleasant consequences. During this celebration, I was thinking chiefly of Paul Steel and all the other dead. If

there was any Winged Victory anywhere, on that day she
was not on our bow, but rising above the graves, the
empty sea, and the homes with empty rooms.

A new point system came by radio, and we found that
only the Captain and I and three enlisted men, in our
whole ship's company, had enough points for release. I
had a long and friendly talk about all this with the Captain, who still looked wretched and had a very slow pulse
and subnormal temperature. He said that he was going
to recommend me for command. "This ship has driven
me crazy," he said, "and it will drive you crazy too in a
few months of going back and barging around those islands; yet I don't think your being given command will
much delay your release." We discussed Mr. Grimm as a
good prospective Executive Officer, and the other officers.
Of course I was touched by the Captain's confidence in
me and grateful for it, after all his insults and all my
impertinences and mistakes. Yet this conversation troubled
me deeply, and I tried to put it all out of my mind until
I got the ship safely into Pearl and squared away for
whatever was coming next.

The next morning, when I came down to the wardroom
after shooting the morning stars and working them out, I
found Mr. Haupt there, eating hugely as usual, and in
high good humor. There was a small radio in the wardroom, and as I sat down, it was blatting out an advertise-
ment from some clothing store in Honolulu. "Get a load
of that, Mr. Smart!" cried Mr. Haupt. "We *made* it! I was
wondering for a moment whether they were advertising
autumn suits in Sitka, Alaska, or in Santiago, Chile!"

But that night of August 15–16, as we approached
Oahu from the southwest, we encountered scores of ships
and I had a wild night on the conn, with Mr. Grimm taking
bearings and working the maneuvering board, and with me

sweating about possible collisions. About 0400, I found myself punch-drunk with it, so I turned the job over to the OD and Mr. Mitchell, with orders to waken me in any trouble. They didn't waken me until dawn, and then I found that our three ships had been set down the coast considerably to the westward. I ate out the OD, then got our ships to the channel entrance on time. We had to wait a long time for a pilot, and when I was about to take her in without one, the Captain appeared, dressed for shore, and made me wait for a pilot. After all, it was still his ship. About noon we were safely moored in a nest of other LSTs. That long voyage, and that long war, were over at last, but as I felt in my weary bones even then, for me the worst part of it all was just coming up.

The Captain promptly went ashore for his medical examination, and while he was gone, I looked up the other two LST skippers, whom I found in one of their ships, holding the post-mortem customary after a long voyage. They had of course expected "Hutch," as they knew him, to join them, and when I told them that he had gone to the hospital and had been in his sack most of the time since Guam, they stared at me and one of them said: "Do you mean to say that you've been the one . . . dishing it out?" I said, "Well, yes." They both laughed, perhaps a bit wryly, because they both knew that I had come through the hawse-hole and had been made a Lieutenant only recently, at Okinawa. Then one of them said, grinning: "Well, you were damned right that morning off Eniwetok."

When the Captain returned, he told me that he had been ordered hospitalized for a lung condition and combat fatigue, and that he would go ashore permanently the next afternoon, leaving me in command that would then be officially confirmed. After I got a liberty party ashore and made arrangements for mail, pay, and a few other immediate necessities, I dumped the ship and the paperwork temporarily on Mr. Grimm and took Messrs. Haupt and Bump to the officers' club for a drink. When we returned, we had a blissful evening of reading our mail. The happiest jolt came to Mr. Haupt, who learned that he was a father, and that although the baby had come slightly early, both it and the mother were thriving. The rice I had got in that hotel in Chicago, or something, had been immediately effective.

The next morning I went to the offices of AdComPhibs-Pac, our bosses, and saw a four-striper and some other officers. They would not accept the applications for release of my three eligible enlisted men and myself on the grounds that they had not yet got orders on the proper forms and procedures.

That afternoon, after packing his gear, getting his commission pennant, and shaking hands with all the officers, the Captain went over the side for the last time. I told him I'd visit him in the hospital. As the boat pulled away, I heard a crack by some enlisted man, and I promptly chewed him out more thoroughly than I had ever done that little job before. That afternoon also I was ordered to put the three enlisted men ashore permanently the next day, and I was informed that I was now Commanding Officer, in accordance with Article 819 of Naval Regulations, and the other officers were moved up as we had anticipated.

During the next six days we were all very busy with the usual work in port, getting stores, parts, fuel, water, repairs, and so on, but I dumped as much of the work as I reasonably could on the new Executive Officer, Mr. Grimm, who went at it with good will. Meanwhile, the back and often the front of my mind were busy with a vital problem of my own. I knew enough about the Navy, and about the situation at that time at Pearl Harbor, to recognize that without vigorous action of some kind by myself, and probably even despite such action, I should very soon be sent westward again, in command of *1122*, and that if I did take her west, my relief from command, and my return to the States for release from the Navy, would be delayed many months. Like millions of other men in all the services, now that the job was done except for some cleaning up that might perhaps be done by the professionals, I was passionately eager to return to my wife, my home, and some kind of normal, productive life and work. I also found myself so tired that even the broken sleep that I could now get for a few nights did not seem to do me much good. On the other hand, once more I did not want to meddle with what seemed to be my fate; I had become more attached than I had known to that ship and her men; once more I felt called upon to deliver whatever skill I had acquired; and not many forty-year-old writers have a chance to command a ship of the United States Navy about to return to the Orient. It was my aching fatigue that proved decisive. Even there in port I was forcing myself every minute, and I did not feel at all confident that I could do that job for months longer without bungling it and without endangering several million dollars' worth of ship and the more than a hundred men (and their families) that had been entrusted to me.

I remember sitting at my little desk with my head on my arms when a mess attendant knocked on the bulkhead beside my curtained door, stood there, and said to me with some of the deep compassion of his race: "Cap'n, Suh, why don' you let me move you' geah into de cabin? You'll be more cool an' comfortable dere." This man was no "sander," no Uncle Tom. His record in other ships contained notations about heroism in action, insubordination, and VD. We had had no trouble with him whatever. "Thank you, son," I said, "but no, don't do that. I'm going to try to get myself relieved of command."

The next morning I went back to the office ashore and saw a Lieutenant Commander who seemed to have enough authority, and who seemed to be impressed by my age and fatigue. He sent me on to another office full of bright young men and weary and cynical older and higher officers. One of the latter said to me: "Captain, I get your point, but you saw that queue outside. They are all Commanding Officers, some of them have more years and stripes than yours, and they are all asking for relief from command. Your former Captain recommended you highly, you have only been in the Pacific a few months this time, and we just don't have any relief skippers for the LSTs. Captain, I'm afraid you're *stuck*." Feeling a bit sick, I said: "Thank you, Sir," and turned away. Then he said, "Look, Captain, it depends somewhat on your orders. If you get orders to go west, come back here and I'll see what I can do for you. I'm not promising a thing." I thanked him again, more warmly, and departed.

Then I went to the hospital to see my Captain, and I had with me a sheaf of papers that he had not signed before leaving the ship. He was in a sack in a crowded quonset hut, and he seemed more rested and cheerful. He had been promoted to Lieutenant Commander, and that comes for merit, not just by date. When I congratulated him on this, he congratulated me, ironically, on my being confirmed in command of *1122*. We chatted about the state of the ship, her officers and men, her prospects, and mine—of which last he took a dim view. We also talked, for the first time in months, about his wife and mine. When I shook his hand and turned away, I knew I'd probably never see him again, and I was sorry.

Then I got a bus and went to an officers' club on the east side of the island, which was spectacularly beautiful. The place was jam-packed with about five hundred officers and maybe ten girls, Waves and nurses. When I had had a swim and was standing, in trunks only, in a crowd at the bar, one of the girls pushed past me, her hair brushed my naked shoulder, and I nearly jumped out of my skin. "Smart," I said to myself, "a few more weeks of this celibacy and you'll be back in sheer, raving adolescence." Presently, after dressing, I got to talking with a regular Navy Commander, and after some shop talk he said: "Mr. Smart, you're in the regular Navy, aren't you?" This was a high compliment, but it also shook me a bit. If I unwittingly sounded that much like a pro, maybe it was high time for me to get back to a typewriter. And yet that thought soon shook me a bit also. I have never been able to think of my old books (which I cannot read) with much pride or pleasure, and the few notes and sketches I had managed to write during the war were clearly worthless. What was I, anyway?

A few days later I took Mr. Grimm with me out to see the ever-hospitable Browns, and I took with me a bottle of whiskey the Captain had given me just before he left the ship, but this time I drank tea only, with Jayne. When I said we had to get back aboard, Bill said: "Take it easy! Take it easy! You're going to have many months more to worry about that ship and her men." Then Jayne looked at me and murmured: "God, I *hope* not. What he needs is about a month in bed." "With Peggy," completed Bill. On the way back to the dock I told Mr. Grimm that if I got relief, he might well see my successor crack up also, and then he'd get command himself. "And that idea," he said grimly, "does not leave me bubbling with delight."

On the morning of August 21, the blow came. An

elegant young Ensign (where, late in 1945, did they find these types?) came aboard, saluted me smartly, and handed me orders to load on a beach near Pearl Harbor, three days later, preparatory to proceeding to such-and-such a port in Japan, which I think was Sasebo. He also handed me an order to attend a meeting of Commanding Officers that day "on future operations." I signed for the damned orders, got on with my work, and then hurried to that meeting, which was filled with men who looked as grim as I felt myself. I forced myself to listen carefully and take notes, because it seemed more than likely that I'd have to execute those orders myself.

As soon as that meeting was over, I hurried to see the officer in Personnel who had told me to return when I got orders. He listened to me without expression, then conferred with some of his junior officers, who then scurried about among their files and papers. After a long wait, one of them returned to me with papers that he said were orders to a certain Lieutenant Gail B. Hood, Executive Officer of LST Such-and-such, to relieve me of the command of LST *1122*. "Hood will kick the bulkhead down," he said. "He has been in the Pacific twenty-two months, and he is expecting stateside leave. You will have to hand him these orders yourself, and you will be responsible for getting him aboard your ship and turning her over to him in the proper manner. His Captain will not love you either. Here also are your own papers of relief of command and transfer for release from active duty."

I thanked him and his superior and then hurried out to find Hood's ship, which was no easy matter. I was immensely relieved, of course, but still anxious. Hood might go back to that personnel officer and work on him with success. I felt only an odd twinge or two, no more, of guilt about playing this trick, if it was that, on the poor devil who was about, he thought, to go home. When I found Hood's ship, he was not aboard, but his Captain received his orders and then, cursing me and the whole Navy with eloquence, promised to deliver them. I told him politely that I'd send a boat for Mr. Hood at 1000 the next morning. When that time approached, I was too busy to leave the ship, so I sent Mr. Bump in one of our boats for the new Captain. When they returned with a serious and able-looking young officer and his gear, I could have shouted "Hallelujah!"

Mr. Hood was very formal and courteous, and meticulous in his attention to all the details of the rather complex operation of the transfer of command of a ship. I installed him in the cabin at once, and although I may have been deceiving myself, I had the comforting impression that his disappointment over not going home had been somewhat assuaged by his pride in becoming the master of a ship. That young man looked good to me, and I felt happy about that, because of all my officers and men. When I suddenly had to move the ship across the harbor, I was very nervous about it, and decided that the ship might well be safer with Mr. Hood. As the job of taking inventory and completing the paper work continued into that night, and I pulled my gear together, all the officers and many of the men kept thinking up ways to help me, kept saying they hated like hell to see me go, and wished all good things to me and to Peggy too. It was very moving, and I found myself stamping all over that ship, and looking into every corner of her, in a high state of nerves.

The next morning, August 23, we held the final ceremony on the weather deck, with all hands in formation, according to the book. I had to read several documents, the new Captain had to read several documents, and the commission pennant was hauled down, and then handed to me by Mr. Grimm. He then stepped forward, saluted the new Captain, and said: "Excuse me, Captain, but many of the officers and men of this ship have come to me and requested permission for all hands to give a personal hand-salute to Mr. Smart, as an officer and a gentleman." The new Captain said: "Certainly," and it was done. From those men, after those months, that was the highest honor I had ever received, or shall receive. My gear was at the Jacob's ladder. I quickly shook hands with all the officers and men who came crowding in there on the quarterdeck. Except for Hilmar Grimm, I have seen none of them since, but during the last twenty years I have wondered about many of them with gratitude, and with hope for their good fortune.

Then I climbed down into the boat and told the boys to shove off, while everyone waved and I waved back. The boat crew that morning were Martin and Hoag, who had pulled me from the drink at Okinawa. We laughed again about that, shook hands and saluted, and I watched them take the boat away. Standing there on that deck, in the middle of that huge and immensely crowded and busy naval base, I felt more freezingly alone, hollow, and empty than I have ever felt in my life.

28

Still cold and numb inside, I went first to the transportation office, which was crowded, and there they told me that since a great many officers and men were applying for transportation to the States, and very little room was available in any kind of vessel, it might well be several weeks before I could be shipped out. Meanwhile they sent me to a BOQ (Bachelor Officers' Quarters) up near the hospital that had a mess attached. As soon as I had left my gear and tried to eat some lunch, I sent a cable or radio to Peggy, telling her that I had been relieved of command on points, was awaiting transportation, and hoped to be home in a month or so. Then I fell on my sack and slept for several hours.

When I awakened, I felt utterly wretched. This was the moment for which Peggy and I, like most of humanity, had struggled and waited for a long time, and now that it had arrived, I found myself too empty, too nonexistent, to enjoy or even to credit it. In an effort to get a grip on something, I thought about my future. From the record, one would say that I was or had been a writer, but now that peculiar visceral-mental activity seemed as remote from myself as juggling or banking. Our farming operations had been liquidated; I knew that in our region, as elsewhere, the farm unit that was economic had grown much larger than anything I could finance; and in any case, I now felt much too exhausted to be able to even imagine my returning to that very hard physical and mental work that has to be carried on about fourteen hours a day. For two years at Choate, long before, I had taught English and enjoyed it, but I had not studied literature systematically for a long time; I did not want to move out of my home to find a teaching job, and that activity now seemed as unreal and as remote from myself as any others I could imagine. If I was anything now, I was a sailor, simply because my whole mind and body had been concentrated on that job so intently, for so long. However, I was now too old for the regular Navy, and even after a long rest, I felt I'd be too feeble for it or for the merchant marine.

This groping, which was probably less rational than it sounds here, then changed into something else, much worse, that is very hard to report—partly, I suppose, because when I try to relive it, as I have done from time to time in the last few months, I begin to succeed, and this experience would frighten anyone. I remember sitting there in that barracks, among other men I did not know or want to know, staring at them and at a long row of bunks and windows, then staring at my own hands, and not believing in any of it. My flickering, implausible, and confused memories of my past before the war, and then even of the war itself, down through the phantom ship and men I had left that very morning, all this, the room I sat in, my own body, and anything I could imagine—it all had no purpose, no meaning, no value, no beauty, and not even any significant ugliness or evil. Its only reality was that of a nightmare of sorts, but it lacked even the vital terror of a nightmare. The only emotion it aroused in me was a cold, sickening disgust. I remember going into the head, staring at my own face in the mirror, and wondering who the hell this guy was, where he had come from, and where he was going. Returning to my sack, I tried to think about Peggy, and to imagine her there before me, or beside me, but somehow I couldn't even do that. When I looked at a snapshot of her in my wallet, I told myself: that's my "wife" all right, I think, a fine woman who used to be my ally, my friend, in some other world, some good world that had vanished or that had never existed, that I was now only imagining. If I ever got back to her in some place, that place, and she in it, would surely be as unreal, as unrelated to me (whatever I was), and as mildly, coldly disgusting as myself, as I sat there, and as that barracks and all the world I should ever know. This was the ultimate freeze, and I lay down on my face, thought about the men I had seen dead on the beaches and in the surf, and wished sincerely, with whatever will I had left, that I too had been killed.

Any good psychiatrist could probably have diagnosed this experience perhaps as a temporary alienation from "reality," with loss of a sense of identity, a "situational neurosis" caused by my incoherent life and by my exhaustion, all triggered by my emotional and disruptive experience on leaving my ship and my mates that morning. To me, this experience is almost more interesting for its philosophical implications. How can we assume that the visions of life that we have when we are "well"—more comfortably and happily "adjusted"—are more valid and true, or more useful to us in the long run, than those we have when we are ill? Perhaps the appalling world in which I lived that afternoon and evening, a world into which I have slipped again from time to time, if less deeply and painfully, is a more inclusive and basic one, and perhaps it is sometimes good for some of us to be reminded of it— if, please, briefly and gently. If this is true, doesn't this

fact support my view that our hopelessly making our little
lives and little worlds as good as we can is the only answer,
and a sufficient one? This experience also suggests to me,
as an occasional reader and even writer of fiction, why
realism, arising from a more or less normal vision of life,
however perceptive and healthy, is so shallow and un-
satisfying. In this century, most of us have reason to know,
from our own experiences, something about the implausi-
bility, the meaninglessness, the permanent mystery, the
horror, and yes, the ravishing beauty of whatever it is that
surrounds the cozy and fragile mental nests that we build
for ourselves. The tellers of the tales that give us more and
better life get outside of the mental suburbs.

The above is written twenty years later. That evening I
was still in that gray, freezing hell. Somehow I pulled myself together enough to go out to the mess hall for supper.
I am not sure, but I think I was helped a little by some
strange kind of pride. Hadn't my first Captain told us, and
hadn't I told other men, that we could accept fear and
get on with the job? This wasn't fear, or at least it wasn't
the same kind of fear, and in its hideous way it was much
worse, but couldn't I still stand and deliver? And didn't
this mean putting on a plausible act of being Lieutenant
C. A. Smart (DV-G) USNR 364363, one more weary
little bastard hanging around Pearl Harbor, hoping to get
home? To me, the men in that messhall were all grisly
little phantoms like myself, putting on acts of being men,
but I have always admired good actors, on or off the
stage. I couldn't eat anything, and across the table there
was a young Ensign who couldn't eat anything either. We
looked at each other and managed to grin, after a fashion.
We went out of that place together, and I said to that
Ensign: "Look, Mister, don't you think that you and I
could use a drink together?"

He said he reckoned we could. I'm not at all sure what happened after that, but I think that we went to the officers' club, had a few together, then decided that we'd be a good deal more safe and comfortable if we bought a bottle and continued in the BOQ, close to our sacks. Of course drinking in that barracks was forbidden, but this Ensign and I didn't give a damn about that. I don't know his name, and I don't think we talked about ourselves, or the Navy, or anything much. That young man may have been well and kind, or he may have been as sick as I was, or worse. I think we just drank silently together, and from time to time just grinned at each other, after a fashion, there in that bar, and then back in our barracks.

Whether he was sick or not, he was certainly kind, because when I awakened, I was in my shorts in my sack, my clothes were all neatly hanging in my locker, and below them there was a bottle of whiskey, half full. The odd thing was that I did not have a hangover, at least of any normal kind. I was just very light-headed, and very stiff and sore all over my body, but especially in the side of my chest. After I had managed to shave, bathe, and dress, I still felt so very odd that I decided to find a sick bay. I was still living in that nightmare of unreality, but now it was not appalling and disgusting, merely funny. The only thing to do was to act normal and take everything for granted. Hadn't I been living in some kind of a dream for nearly four years? Somehow I found the sick bay, nearby, and all I remember about that is the Pharmacist's Mate's saying cheerfully: "Good morning, Sir. Not feeling too well? You don't remember? You fell down a thirty-foot ladder, just outside that BOQ, and you're lucky you didn't break your neck. Now let me take a look at you." By "ladder" he meant a stairway. At some point during his investigation of my person, I must have fainted dead away. I have only a dim memory of being hauled around on a stretcher and put under an X-ray machine.

When I came to, more or less, I was in a quonset hut full of other men, my chest was tightly taped, and a Wave Pharmacist's Mate was fussing over me. She told me that it was August 26, which meant that I had been unconscious for three days. She said that I had a broken rib and pneumonia, and she promised to write a reassuring note to my wife. I went back to sleep, and I was probably under sedation. Two days later, I found my brain relatively clear, and my body strong enough, despite a sharp pain when I coughed and very sore arms and buttocks from injections, to stagger to the head and with great difficulty to shave. None of this mattered at all, because to my immense relief I had come almost entirely out of that nightmare, and was now back in the normal world.

Now came another shock. Rejoicing in my sanity and trying to strengthen it, I spoke to several of the other men there, all naval officers, first in the head and then from my bed. In each and every case, the man I spoke to looked away and did not answer me. For some reason quite unknown to me, I was a pariah. Had I screamed in pain? Quite possibly, but if I had, I wasn't ashamed of that, and I had seen men scream in pain without any sailors present responding with anything but sympathy. They scorned only men trying to duck out of dangerous jobs. Had I been mistaken for some other officer with an unsavory record? That seemed equally implausible. Had my mental collapse, or whatever it had been, now taken the form of paranoia, with delusions of persecution? This idea really frightened me again, so I kept on trying to strike up conversations, but still, every single time, I was given the deep freeze. This was no delusion, a discovery that relieved me, but I still found the situation distinctly unpleasant.

Lying there alone in that crowd of heroes, I stared at the ceiling and finally decided that the cause of this disagreeable episode was much less important than my own response to it. My own streak of vanity had long annoyed me, and now that it was hurt again in this peculiar fashion, wasn't this a good chance finally to get rid of it? If I was in fact "an officer and a gentleman," was I also one of the millions of American creampuffs who desperately need to be popular, to be loved? Presently I found myself thinking, with what felt like complete honesty: *the hell with it;* then I found myself looking at the men around me with a fresh eye, mildly curious and even amused. Then I returned to sleep.

That this "conversion," as I called it to myself, was not superficial was further indicated by my response to what happened next. The doctors and nurses kept pumping me full of penicillin and sulfa drugs until my fever went down, but the adhesive around my chest raised large blood blisters that were very uncomfortable for a while, and X-rays showed that I had not recovered full use of my left lung. To correct this, I was required regularly to blow into a rubber glove and inflate it. When I was doing this, the men around me made all kinds of ingenious and obscene jokes about it, introduced themselves, and began to call me "Pappy"! Their attitude toward me was now even more cordial and friendly that it had previously been cold and hostile. They insisted on chattering with me even more than my strength would permit me to enjoy. After they had discovered my civilian trade, one of them went to the library, came back crowing with a copy of *R.F.D.,* and insisted on reading aloud, until I stopped him, the more intimate passages. I heard one lad say: "Brother, would I like to latch on to some tomato like this Peggy!" During the long days that followed, I was bathed in solicitude and affection by a crowd of delightful and interesting young men. This was pleasant, of course, but what pleased me more was the fact that it did not mean too much to me. When I thought once of asking them why I had been a pariah at first, and why they had changed their minds about me, I found I didn't really care, and could honestly say again: the hell with it.

That I was not the only man on the way home from war who was returning by way of his private little hell was made clear enough in that quonset hut. At one end of it there was one little room walled off, and one morning I saw in the bed in that room a man with his throat heavily bandaged; and in the room with him there sat a sailor armed with a pistol. The patient was sitting up in bed reading a newspaper, a fact that I remembered with surprise when I learned that the night before, this man had cut his throat from ear to ear. We had among us, as a patient, a very sensitive and intelligent neurosurgeon named Dr. Donald, from Fall River, and when I asked him about the newspaper the morning after, he told me that the would-be suicide had undoubtedly got great temporary relief from the attempt, but would probably slip back, and in a few weeks make another attempt. One day when some of us were hauled out to a fine picnic luncheon on a beach owned by some ranchers named Carter, I had more talks with Dr. Donald. I was still frightened by my own brief descent into hell on August 23, so I asked him whether he thought I'd get drunk and try to break my neck again. He looked at me with a strange, sad smile and said: "Probably, Pappy, but I don't think certainly, or at all successfully. You have been weakened and disoriented, like most of us, but you have such zest, and enough detachment to ask me that question."

As I grew stronger, I grew frantic to go home, especially

when I heard that the *Saratoga* had sailed for the States with thirty-five hundred passengers on the flight deck and in the passageways. At this time I got an astonishingly friendly letter from my last Captain, who had been moved to Camp Erdman, a rest camp, and who suggested that I join him there if I had to wait for transportation. When I was finally released from the hospital, I went to the transportation office before doing anything about that camp, and with great good luck I got a place in SS *Mission Soledad*, a merchant tanker sailing for some unspecified port in the States on September 12.

29

Those last fifteen days, until their end, were mostly a blank of waiting and moving on. A last desperate climb up the Jacob's ladder of a ship that seemed to me, with my sore chest, as high as the Empire State Building. Sleeping, eating with merchant officers and with naval flyers, sleeping again. The Golden Gate, lying in a hotel room with a horribly stiff neck, finally getting orders and catching a train to Chicago. Great Lakes again, Peggy on the telephone on her birthday, standing in queues, endless papers, my idiocy in not having my hernia repaired then and there.

Finally, finally, in the grim old railroad station of Columbus, Ohio, standing by a pillar looking for me, there was my Peggy, thin but full of life that flowed into me.

Driving down into our own blue hills on that misty autumn morning, we decided to call at once on our old friends Bob and Edith Steel, the parents of Paul Steel, for whom all hope had been given up. This wasn't courtesy; it was a kind of compulsion. Bob and Edith were still living, at that time, in their big old house on their fine, big farm—in the orchard of which, on the back of our own hill, Peggy and I had decided to get married. Bob was not at home, and while we were waiting for Edith we saw on the floor, just inside the front door, Paul's trunk, which (we learned later) had arrived just that morning from the War Department. My blood froze. My God, what was *I* doing, standing there alive, with much of a full life behind me, looking at that lifeless trunk with a name painted on it? When Edith appeared, she greeted us gallantly, but her haggard face was wet. There were few or no words for that moment, and we soon went home.

That evening, I went with our niece Betsey out to the barn, where she milked our last remaining cow, and then poured out at least half of that precious milk for the twenty-one cats that she and the other Little Women and Peggy had been simply unable to drown. Later Peggy and I walked out our front drive together, hand in hand, under the great trees, and looked at the hills and the sky. When we had been together, we had done that for ten years, crowding a good deal of life into them, and we hoped to have a good many more years together. A few days later, I bought some civilian clothes, and when I put them on, they seemed as strange and silly to me as my first gob suit had seemed at Great Lakes. Then my mental health and our bank account both suggested that I had better get a job, and after four months of sleeping and writing letters, I got a good one. Some claim that "His eye is on the sparrow."

For twenty years, like most veterans and other people, I have gone about looking and acting more or less as though I believed that human existence made some sense. I do believe that, but whatever sense, whatever truth, goodness, and beauty appear are fought for and gained only by the men and women, usually humble, like those you have seen in these pages, who love life and who are intent on doing, within their limits, good jobs of it.

This book was composed on
the Linotype in Times Roman,
which was designed by Stanley
Morison for the London *Times*,
and first used in that newspaper.
Its masculine simplicity,
directness of design, and
excellent color make it
exceptionally useful for
periodicals and general
commercial work. The basic
design objective of maximum
legibility in minimum space has
resulted in the large
letter-structure that makes each
point size seem the equivalent
of a size larger in most other
types.

Typography and design by
Charles Curtis